The Garden of Divine Songs

and Collected Poetry of

Hryhory Skovoroda

TRANSLATED BY MICHAEL M. NAYDAN

WITH AN INTRODUCTION BY VALERY SHEVCHUK

TRANSLATIONS EDITED BY OLHA TYTARENKO

GLAGOSLAV PUBLICATIONS

The Garden of Divine Songs
and Collected Poetry of Hryhory Skovoroda

by Hryhory Skovoroda

Translated by **Michael M. Naydan**
With an introduction by Valery Shevchuk
Translations Edited by Olha Tytarenko

The cover shows a detail from *DNA of Ukraine* by
Mykola Kumanovsky from the Woskob Private Collection

Publishers Maxim Hodak & Max Mendor

© 2015, Michael M. Naydan

© 2016, Glagoslav Publications, United Kingdom

Glagoslav Publications Ltd
88-90 Hatton Garden
EC1N 8PN London
United Kingdom

www.glagoslav.com

ISBN: 978-1-91141-403-2

This book is in copyright. No part of this publication may be reproduced, stored in a retrieval system or transmitted in any form or by any means without the prior permission in writing of the publisher, nor be otherwise circulated in any form of binding or cover other than that in which it is published without a similar condition, including this condition, being imposed on the subsequent purchaser.

The Garden of Divine Songs

and Collected Poetry of

Hryhory Skovoroda

TRANSLATED BY MICHAEL M. NAYDAN

WITH AN INTRODUCTION BY VALERY SHEVCHUK

TRANSLATIONS EDITED BY OLHA TYTARENKO

*This translation is dedicated to
Liliana Ursu, a poet who in our time
walks the same path as Skovoroda.*

Many thanks to the Woskob family for granting permission to use the artwork of Mykola Kumanovsky entitled "DNA of Ukraine" from their private collection of art for the cover of this book.

Hryhory Skovoroda

(1722-1794)

A note from the editor and translator

The preeminent Ukrainian philosopher and poet Hryhory Skovoroda (1722-1794) strikes me profoundly as a man who found the truth, who found love, who found happiness, all in a simple and rustic way of life with just the clothes on his back and a knapsack containing a Bible. He dedicated his life to the pursuit of knowledge and through that knowledge—wisdom. He saw the interconnectedness of all things, of God with man and nature, of man with nature, of past civilizations with the present. Skovoroda saw God's holy truth as a continuum stretching from the biblical times of the ancient Hebrews and the greatest thinkers of Ancient Greece and Rome—to his contemporary times. Skovoroda, too, saw the Old Testament of the Bible as one great continuum with the New. His is the God of Abraham as well as the God of Christ. Both his Old and New Testament scholarship are formidable in his logical and intuitive pursuit to extrapolate this unity.

It is not for nothing that Skovoroda has been called the Ukrainian Socrates, for he spent most of his life teaching and giving to others freely to help them find their way to God and true happiness. Skovoroda was the planter of the seeds of wisdom that he found in the good books and in his life experiences. At the same time that

Kant was shifting focus to the purely rational in neighboring Western Europe, Skovoroda was living his intuitive philosophy of the heart and explicating it to anyone who would listen. In his time Skovoroda appealed to all strata of society, from the poorest peasant to the wealthiest landowners and the most highly educated clergy, for he treated everyone as a special creation and as equal in the eyes of God. This unassuming, learned genius, who felt most at peace in the wilds of nature, lived his life as he preached it, at total peace with himself.

This first volume in a planned three-volume edition of the selected works of Skovoroda, whom I once heard Nobel Prize winning poet Joseph Brodsky call "the first great Slavic poet," has been a labor of love for everyone involved in the task. Skovoroda's life and thought have fascinated such luminaries of the Slavic literary world as Russian writers Leo Tolstoy and Andrei Bely, and master 20th-century Ukrainian poet Pavlo Tychyna. The impact of Skovoroda in his native Ukraine has transcended legend. This series of volumes will introduce this great poet and thinker to a wider audience and, hopefully, will generate additional interest in one of the greatest Orthodox religious thinkers of his time. The entire project has taken longer than expected since its inception partly because of the complexity of the language of the original texts as well as its ever-increasing scope. The planned three volumes will contain translations of all of Skovoroda's extant poetry in the first volume, all of his extant correspondence in the second, and seven of his most seminal philosophical treatises in the third. Many of his letters border on the homiletic and comprise brilliant lyrically philosophical treatises in miniature. They also offer a glimpse into the warm and profound friendship that Skovoroda shared with his disciple Mykhailo Kovalynsky, who is largely responsible for conserving Skovoroda's writings for posterity. Several of the poems, especially a number from the *Garden of Divine Songs* cycle and the poem "On the Holy Supper, Or Eternity," are Ukrainian literary Baroque masterpieces of the metaphysical.

Since Skovoroda knew the Bible so thoroughly in so many languages, including Old Church Slavic, Ancient Greek, Ancient Hebrew, and Latin, identification of Biblical quotations, as a result of variations in translation across languages and cultures, presents a significant problem for translators.[1] Leonid Ushkalov has done an admirable job of identifying Biblical sources in his complete works edition of Skovoroda.

I owe a great debt of gratitude to the editors of the 1973 two-volume collected works edition of Skovoroda—*Povne zibrannia tvoriv* (Kyiv) for having managed to publish such a profoundly spiritual author in the rather dismal times of the then virulently anti-religious Soviet Union. Another great debt is owed to the translators of Skovoroda into modern Ukrainian—Valery Shevchuk and Maria Kashuba, who have made my task easier as editor. To resolve numerous sticky wickets I have been able to check these English translations against the 1994 two-volume modern Ukrainian edition of Skovoroda: *Hryhorii Skovoroda: Tvory v dvokh tomakh* (Kyiv) as well as against the most comprehensive and authoritative volume to date of

---

1   See George Shevelov's article "Prolegomena to Studies of Skovoroda's Language and Style" (pp. 93-132) in Richard H. Marshall, Jr. and Thomas E. Bird, ed. *Hryhorij Savyc Skovoroda: An Anthology of Critical Articles* (Toronto and Edmonton: Canadian Institute of Ukrainian Studies Press, 1994) for a revealing discussion of Skovoroda's probable sources and method for biblical quotation.

Skovoroda's writings edited by Leonid Ushkalov—*Hryhorii Skovoroda: Povna akademichna zbirka tvoriv* (Kharkiv: "Maidan" Publishers, 2011). The notes in all of these modern editions of Skovoroda have been extraordinarily useful. I am especially grateful to Valery Shevchuk, the preeminent Ukrainian writer and one of the leading experts on the life and works of Skovoroda in the world, for providing such a comprehensive and thoughtful introduction to this volume.

The main goal in these translations has been to present the great thinker and poet Skovoroda in an accessible idiom in English while maintaining the poeticality along with some of the archaic feel in the originals. In the poetry, I have tried to include natural end rhymes whenever possible and internal rhymes (sometimes in a compensatory way) in order to convey Skovoroda's poeticality without drastically changing his essential meaning. Skovoroda does not, in fact, always use end rhymes (Song No. 3, for example as well as in many of the poems outside of the 30 contained in *The Garden of Divine Songs*). Words in brackets were added for the sake of rhymes and are not in the original texts. This will allow for more precise quotation for scholars yet permit readers to experience the playfulness of Skovoroda's style. While Skovoroda's writings may seem archaic to a modern speaker of Ukrainian or Russian, they were written in the scholarly idiom of the philosopher-poet's time and function as a testimony to the poet-philosopher's extraordinarily expansive and lucid mind.

Acknowledgments

A number of people have been generous with their assistance on the translation project, and I want to take the opportunity to express my gratitude to several of them. I am grateful to William Schmalstieg for taking the time to share his expertise on Old Church Slavic with me to clear up a number of my questions. Adrian Wanner was kind enough to check a number of Latin passages for me. Mykola Riabchuk elucidated a number of my questions on translation from Ukrainian, particularly in the introduction to the volume. My gratitude to Richard Gustafson for introducing me to Skovoroda's thought in graduate school at Columbia University in his fine seminar on Russian and Slavic thought, and to Ukrainian poet Vasyl Barka who, in living the life of a neo-Skovorodian philosopher-poet himself, so effectively conveyed the essence of Skovoroda to me at an early stage in my career. Extra special thanks to Olha Tytarenko for her meticulous editorial comments on the final version of the manuscript, which greatly improved the translations. My gratitude, too, to my daughter Lila Naydan for her quite useful comments on the final versions of the English of my poetry translations. I, of course, am responsible for any errors or omissions. Ukrainian writer and philosophy scholar Oksana Zabuzhko is most responsible for using her powers of persuasion to convince me to tackle this project. I am also grateful to Svitlana Kobets,

Steve Scherer and John Fizer for moral support, and to my mother Anna Naydan for having constantly given me gentle urgings over time to complete the project. Special thanks to Philip Winsor of The Pennsylvania State University Press for his early support of the project.

I also owe a great debt of gratitude to the following individuals and organizations, who so kindly supported both a conference celebrating the 200-year anniversary of Skovoroda's death at The Pennsylvania State University in 1994, whose proceedings have been published in 1998 as a special issue of *Journal of Ukrainian Studies*, as well as this publication project with their contributions: the Woskob Family Endowment in Ukrainian Studies and the Myroslawa and Iwan Iwanciw Fund for Ukrainian Studies, both at The Pennsylvania State University, the Self-Reliance Federal Credit Union (New York), Self-Reliance Federal Credit Union (Newark, N.J.), Self-Reliance Federal Credit Union (Hartford, Conn.), Ukrainian Fraternal Association, Providence Association of Ukrainian Catholics in America, Ukrainian Future Credit Union (Warren, Mich.), Rochester Ukrainian Federal Credit Union, and Ukrainian Credit Union (Minneapolis); and Mr. Peter and Mrs. Katerine Caruk, Ms. Mary Chimow, Mr. Longen and Mrs. Marian Chuchman, Dr. Bohdan Chudio, Mr. Adrian Dolinsky, Mr. Paul and Mrs. Irene Dzul, Ms. Olga Fedirko, Mr. Joseph Gellner, Mr. Michael Hlady, Mr. Michael and Mrs. Mary Hojsan, Ms. Maria Iskiw, Ms. Daria Kozak, Mr. Wasyl and Mrs. Anna Makuch, Mr. John Orichosky, Mr. Jaroslav and Mrs. Jaroslava Panchuk, Dr. Julian and Mrs. Myroslawa Pawlyszyn, Mr. Michael Tansky, Mr. Dmytro and Mrs. Helen Tataryn, Ms. Lana Tonkoschkur, Mr. Peter Twerdochlib, Mr. George and Mrs. Nina Woskob, Mr. Roman Zaharchuk, Mr. Carl Zapotny, and other anonymous donors.

A Note on Transliteration

I have opted for the Library of Congress transliteration throughout the volume. Only parenthetical words and important quotations in Greek and Latin are left in the body of the texts, while everything else, whether originally in Old Church Slavic, Latin or Greek, has been translated into English. Translations of all the parenthetical expressions and quotations are glossed in footnotes or in brackets in the text. I use the principle of simplifying names for an English-speaking audience in the body of the text. Thus "Hryhory" instead of the transliterated "Hryhorii" or "Hryhorij." I have also opted for Ukrainian versions of names. Thus "Hryhory" instead of "Gregory" or the Russian "Grigory." "Mykhailo" instead of "Michael" or the Russian "Mikhail." And place names such as "Kharkiv" in Ukrainian instead of the Russian "Kharkov."

– Michael M. Naydan, *Woskob Family*
Professor of Ukrainian Studies
The Pennsylvania State University

Introduction

THE LIFE AND WORKS OF HRYHORY SKOVORODA
by Valery Shevchuk

To comprehend the phenomenon of Hryhory Skovoroda, one must characterize his life and his philosophical views both individually as well as in their interrelatedness, that is, in the central ideas that he worked out in his dialogues and treatises, as well as his literary activity. All these things comprise a single constellation, a single lesson, produced in various forms. Skovoroda lived as he taught. He taught through wisdom and, eventually, created his own teachings in images, with the aid of the art of the word, of music, of painting.

The life of Skovoroda now amazes us, because a roofless existence for the contemporary intellect is, in fact, unimaginable. Even in his time this impressed his contemporaries, in fact astonished them. Nevertheless it was the original mark of a special sphere of Ukrainian society called "wandering deacons," "scholastics"—a unique variety of European vagantes.[2] Wandering deacons and scholastics of the 17th and 18th centuries

---

2   Vagantes (from the Latin) were scholar monks who wandered about Germany, France, England, and Northern Italy from the 11th to the 14th centuries.

took education to the people. As a rule they were teachers in primary schools—these were people with an aesthetics and sensitivity transmitted from the Kyiv Mohyla Academy. They not only taught children in schools, moving from one town to another, but they also cherished poetry. They were transcribers and creators of manuscript books—they created the special province of so-called "deacon's poetry," wrote spiritual cantos and secular works—with a libertine and sometimes even with obscene content. They did not spurn love and meditative poetry. They wrote epitaphs and epigraphs by request, poems in honor of this or that person, and they especially loved to write humoristic and satiric verses. They just never stayed in one place, and similar to the vagantes, wandered about Ukraine, stopping over at schools. They were in close contact with musicians of their era (the lofts where the blind minstrels lived were most often in the same building where the school was). These people were quite useful to society and sensed the significance of their mission, which one of the best such poets of the 19th century, Petro Popovych-Huchensky, proclaimed:

> Since you've forgotten, ladies and gentlemen,
> about us and God,
> We will leave you, to take a different road.
> And with what will the Lord's church be decorated,
> What, mankind, will your soul exalt?
> The Lord's church shines from hymns read aloud,
> And the reading-singing flourishes in gems ...[3]

---

3   *Antolohiia ukrains'koi poezii*, I (Kyiv, 1984), 194.

Thus, by his way of life, Hryhory Skovoroda reminds us of that very cultural stratum of the society of the time: only he, Skovoroda, stood as though on a higher echelon: where the itinerant deacons and scholastics were instructors of the lower school, Skovoroda instructed the higher; where the former were silly and frolicsome, Skovoroda, perhaps, was too dignified and even austere. In this he reminds us of his distant predecessor—the Ukrainian polemicist of the end of the 16th and beginning of the 17th centuries—Ivan Vyshensky, but without the latter's intolerance, because all of Skovoroda's creativity and system of thinking were humanized, and he didn't scorn or curse the culture and literature of antiquity like Vyshensky, but knew it profoundly and made use of it enthusiastically. In the times when Skovoroda lived, the itinerant deacons had left or were leaving the stage of life—by edict of the conventionally Ukrainophobic Russian tsarina Catherine II, who had banned them from traveling. Steadily they were mutated into half literate and half-drunken stammerers, whom Hryhory Kvitka-Osnovnianenko and Nikolai Gogol later ridiculed *kepkuvaly*. Skovoroda himself was like the loving embodiment of the tradition and old culture that in his time had already begun to be reborn; fate allowed it, just as it did to the founder of the modern Ukrainian literary language Ivan Kotlyarevsky, the author of the mock-epic *Eneida* in vernacular Ukrainian, to actualize in Ukrainian culture its entire great period, which we call the literature of the Ukrainian Baroque, and to consummate it with a mighty flash, which in its own way ignited new generations.

Now a brief outline of the life of Skovoroda. Born of a simple Kozak[4] family, from his early childhood years he

---

4   I use "Kozak" instead of the spelling "Cossack" in order to

exhibited extraordinary gifts. Fortunately, the Kyiv Mohyla Academy opened its doors to all gifted children, regardless of the property standing of the parents. There both poor and rich studied. Also, a student was allowed once he entered, to terminate his studies without completing them. Sava Skovoroda sent his son to Kyiv because everyone was drawn there who had the unrestrained gravitation to knowledge and scholarly pursuits. Hryhory—a child with an extraordinary memory—was drawn to poetry, music, singing, painting—all subjects taught at the Academy. Of course the choir director received him into the academic choir: We have no doubts that Skovoroda took an active part in theatrical performances that were organized there, because where else would he acquire so many aphoristic locutions about the theater; that he took an active part in the re-creations—artistically performed graduation ceremonies at the end of the second year. At that time in poetics class the young Skovoroda acquired knowledge of the theory of poetry and practical conventions in metrics, and there he also studied ancient Hebrew, Greek, and first and foremost Latin, immersing himself in philosophy. He

---

differentiate from the Russian Cossack troops in the tsar's service. The Ukrainian Kozaks were mostly former serfs who became fighters for freedom in the steppes against the Russians, Poles and Turks. They were eventually banned and eliminated by Russian rulers Peter I and Catherine II, the latter of whom had them forcibly resettled in Russian territory in order to weaken them. It is unfortunate that in Western culture the appellation "Cossack" seems to suggest marauding pillagers. The Ukrainian Kozaks did venture out in attacks against enemies, but for the most part were a highly religious group (Orthodox Christian) with a strict code of ethics and a democratic system for choosing their leaders. For a discussion of the Ukrainian Kozaks I would recommend Orest Subtelny's *Ukraine: A History*, 2nd ed. (Toronto: U. of Toronto Press, 1994). [Ed.]

read his favorites: Aristotle, Plato, Plutarch, Philo,[5] Cicero, Lucian,[6] Origen,[7] and Erasmus of Rotterdam—all this opened up a wide world for the youth. Finally, for him, like many of his contemporaries, the Kyivan schooling turned out to be too limited and he decided to travel to Western Europe. But before he left he sang for a time in the tsar's a cappella choir in Petersburg, from which he escaped the first chance he had, because the courtly life for his free-spirited soul was reprehensible; a recollection of that life became his phantasmagoric "Dream": "I can't take this stench and awful savagery and with horror, turning away my eyes, I left" (II, 429). He had no wish to stroke the nobleman and tsarist leaders. Thus he travelled to a distant world, to Hungary and to other European lands where he studied (particularly in the University in Halle, Germany), afterward he returned to Ukraine, and when from the distance he saw the wooden church bell tower in his native village, he sensed his heart nearly stop in his chest.

Chronologically the events of his life occurred as follows: he was born in 1722; 1734-1753 with interruptions, he studied at the Kyiv-Mohyla Academy; a singer in the court a cappella choir in Petersburg 1741-1744; in 1745 he returned to the Kyiv Mohyla Academy, that same year he travelled to Hungary (1745-1750). Finally, after returning in 1750-1751, he taught poetics in the Pereyaslav Collegium.

The storyistorija, the way it was played out at the Collegium, had primary meaning for the further fate of

---

[5] Philo Judaeus. Hellenistic Jewish philosopher who lived in the 1st century AD, who combined Judaism with Platonism.

[6] Greek satirist and sceptic from the 2nd century AD.

[7] 3rd century Christian theologian (†254? AD), who advanced Christian philosophy on Platonic lines.

Hryhory Skovoroda. At that time he was 29, taught poetics, and, as was customary, was supposed to prepare his course on this subject, but the Bishop of Pereyaslav Nikodym Srebnytsky, also a student of the Kyiv Academy, for some reason sharply criticized his poetics for its innovations in syllabic versification. Many scholars have noted this incident, but few have noticed that Skovoroda recalls these events in a letter to his pupil Mykhailo Kovalynsky (written in the first half of 1764): "I immediately began to think in this way: the Pereyaslav mice were the reason that they expelled me from the seminary with great unpleasantries" (II, 338-9). One might ask, what kind of mice? Why were they the cause of his being expelled? Just one conclusion is possible with a single answer: obviously the mice chewed up the prepared poetics course, and Skovoroda, without having time to prepare a new one, began to teach poetics without a textbook, which, in practical terms, certainly could not have been appreciated by the bishop, a student of the Academy who justifiably demanded that they teach the subject in the way that was customary. In general, this question deserves a more in-depth analysis, for the unlocking, in my opinion, of one of the keys to understanding the phenomenon of Skovoroda. The poetics written by Hryhory Skovoroda, thus, is considered not to be extant. His biographer Kovalynsky announced that Skovoroda put together "a primer on poetry and a practical guide to the art of poetics" in such an innovative way that the bishop considered it strange and inappropriate in relation to what had been the previous custom. The riddle has attracted scholars, afterward a number of hypotheses were posited, at times, utterly fantastic, as, for example, the idea that Skovoroda slavishly copied the system of the Russian versifier Mikhail Lomonosov, despite the fact that there are no traces of the use of Lomonosov's system on the poetic practice of the thinker. Regarding Skovoroda's "primer on poetry and practical guide to its art," we have only a single reliable source noted by Kovalynsky: they were from the traditionally used ones—"the simplest and best understood ones for students and gave a completely new and accurate understanding of it" (II, 441). The first thing that strikes you on reading this announcement is that the biographer clearly differentiates between the "primer on poetry" and "practical guide." The "primer" has surely been lost—there was, from all evidence, a theoretical part of the course from which the thinker lectured; perhaps the above-mentioned mice ate not the poetics but rather the "primer," and here I should say more about it. On the other hand, the "practical guide to the art of poetry," in my opinion, is extant—this was nothing other than the versified examples of the art of poetry with which Skovoroda in practical terms pointed out possible poetic meters that had been cultivated in Ukrainian poetry over the course of the century. I will be so bold as to articulate that these poems were extant and entered his poetic collection *Garden of Divine Songs*. The entire collection at that time was still not complete; the poet was perfecting it while he was already working at the Kharkiv Collegium (from 1759) and afterward he created his own highly original primer of poetry, therefore his collection *Garden Of Divine Songs* was conceived in universal terms. First of all, as it already seemed, this was a universal, popularized expression of the views of the thinker in poetic form, and secondly—this is true, as an analysis of the works included attests. The "practical guide to the art of poetry," that is, these verses, gives an understanding of all the possible meters and strophic patterns of Ukrainian poetry of that time. And, in fact, none of the 30 poems of the collection duplicate each other rhythmically, and each is written not only differently, but each clearly gives examples of the most multi-faceted structure of the work. Moreover, the poet does not only in practical terms fix existing poetic forms of the Ukrainian Baroque, but also introduces in them an entire series of innovations and propositions, pointing out that one can vary the strophe, rhyme and alternate various types of meters. From this perspective, the collection *Garden of Divine Songs* is utterly unique. And I will now attempt to prove this. The poet nowhere in his collection repeats one and the same strophic structure, and this could not have been a coincidence: we see here the author's conscious intent, and there could only be one reason for the author to construct it this way: his *Garden of Divine Songs* must have been a "practical guide to the art of poetry," since in a relatively small book of 30 poems, we clearly observe a rather complex system of strophic structure, and only a few of the songs are written simply in a traditional way. All possible types of syllabic verse are used there—of 4, 5, 6, 8, 9, 10, 11, 12, 13, 14, 15 and 16 syllables in length. The only one absent is a purely Leonine line (5-5-6) with internal rhyme, which was quite widespread in the poetry of the Ukrainian Baroque, but the element of that line (especially internal rhyme) is used quite often, also the Sapphic strophe is used creatively, and in song #8, the same Sapphic strophe (rhymed, it is understood, that is adapted to Slavic poetics). Skovoroda to a great degree takes advantage of not only the formal accomplishments of academic poetry that was created according to traditional poetics, but most of all the so-called "songs of the world," that is, he borrows the practice of poetry that comes from beyond the borders of the rules of Kyivan poetics, and it developed independently;

true, not without the reckoning of Academic meter. This poetry closely merged with native Ukrainian folk song. One other interesting characteristic: the poet widely uses an eight-line poem that was naturally tonic, the fact of which makes his verse quite close to the syllabo-tonic, but this does not mean that Skovoroda introduced the syllabo-tonic system. The practice of rephrasing the songs of Skovoroda by Vasily Kapnist can attest to the fact that in the second half of the 18th century the syllabic system of poetics no longer satisfied the reading public, nor did the bookish form of the Ukrainian language, which Skovoroda used in his poetry. Therefore Kapnist decided to interpret the verse of Skovoroda according to the precepts of Mikhail Lomonosov, and to make the language of the songs closer to Russian—a tendency rather widespread at that time; in fact, we also find it in the philosophical work of Skovoroda himself.

The poet introduces anew into poetic practice a series of innovative alternating rhymes, the alternation of male and female rhymes, and in a considerably more far-reaching way than his predecessors, he makes use of internal rhyme. We can with complete assuredness say that not in a single poet of the Ukrainian Baroque, even such masterful versifiers as Ivan Ornovsky and Pylyp Orlyk, do we find such rhythmic or strophic variety as in Skovoroda. Therefore, before us is a truly original poetics in examples, an anthology of the verse meters known to Ukrainian literature of the baroque, which Hryhory Skovoroda, as a pedagogue by calling, could use to aid in the teaching of the art (nauka) of poetry to young people. One other thing is important. The collection *Garden of Divine Songs*, as scholars assert, was assembled from the 1750s through 1785, although the greater part of the poems was written in the 1760s. When we recall that Skovoroda taught poetics in Pereyaslav in 1751, and from 1759 was a teacher of versification in the Kharkiv Collegium, we have the basis to prove that "the practical guide to the art of poetry" created in Pereyaslav was only the embryo of a completely worked out system, that is fixed in this collection, therefore during the time of his teaching at the Kharkiv Gymnasium, this system of versification was nearly formed, and in later years, while conducting a wandering life, but dreaming of returning to his beloved teaching, the thinker perfected it, and the year 1785 can serve as the end of this work. On the other hand, this collection was, as we have said above, a poetic compendium of Skovoroda's philosophical ideas, just as his *Kharkiv Tales* are a collection of these ideas in parable form, and this dualism is not mutually contradictory. Recall his words from "Conversations with Five Travelers about True Happiness in Life": "There are two small loaves, two buildings and two pairs of clothing: two kinds of everything in pairs" (II, 353). Thus *Garden of Divine Songs* is as though it were two buildings: one—the exposition of thoughts, the other "a practical guide to the art of poetry."

To make my assertion more persuasive, allow me to examine the basic motifs of *Garden of Divine Songs*. For it is a cycle in which the main ideas, which later create the basis of Skovoroda's philosophical treatises, have already begun to be formulated, or, vice versa: the thoughts of the philosophical treatises could have flowed into the poetry.

The idea of the first song is that he who lives by evil brings about a living death; a hunger burns the soul of such a living man, and he who takes on the yoke of goodness—a light burden—lives as a pure soul. In the second song the poet calls to keep yourself above the vanity of insignificant things, in order to renew joy like a swift flying eagle. In the third song, he who overcomes sorrow and whose soul becomes a garden that bears fruit is glorified. In the fourth song it is stated that the spirit of freedom gives birth to us ourselves. The fifth song declares that recognizing the "heavenly mystery," a human being grows up into a perfect person. In the sixth song, the theme is about the seed that, having rotted, gives buds and a hundred years of fruit, i.e., a human song creates a living action of the world through unhappiness, undergoing even death. In the eighth song, an African deer, wounded by poison, rushes to the mountains to find a healing spring to become whole again (one of the favorite symbolic images of Skovoroda's philosophy). The ninth and tenth songs speak of human passion and vain-thinking, which ruin a person, about the insatiable accumulation of wealth—which forever provokes death. Who withstands death? "He whose conscience is crystal clear!" The poet answers.

Even from an analysis of the first ten poems of *Garden of Divine Songs* we may conclude that the poet places before us a triangle: evil (a crooked path), which brings illusory satisfaction, and then sadness, sorrow, dissatisfaction; goodness (the narrow path), which is difficult to attain, but which brings spiritual joy, peace and satisfaction; and a person, who stands at the crossroads and has to choose where to go.

This question of where a person should go to become purified, how he or she should acquire not rank, riches or material wealth, but rather a spiritual peace, joy and illumination, became one of the main ideas of not only the poetry of Skovoroda, but also of his fables, and later all of his philosophical treatises.

The next ten songs continue to develop the philosophical ideas of Skovoroda. In the 11th song he counterposes the human (material) and the spiritual (ideal, God) and speaks of the eternal competition between these two principles. The 12th song professes the fact that human civilization with its cities and riches is antithetical to nature and to humankind in general, people must go "to live in the field," that is, to come closer to nature and therefore to God. Song #13 continues this theme and is a panegyric to nature, while cities with their artificial civilization are antithetical. Song #14 teaches the ephemerality and illusoriness of the world, of fame, and proclaims that it would be better to live in a desert.

In the 15th song the poet again returns to the theme of death, but in an original way: death is the end of earthly sagacity and the beginning of heavenly glory, and afterward, just as if it were the continuation of this theme—resurrection, the feeling of a pure sky (song 16). The next poem is an escape from a sea of life that seethes like the Red Sea, again into quietude, into peacefulness, into nature (songs 17 and 18). However, "accursed boredom" comes to the hero here, it is about the need to struggle with it with God's help (song 19). Song 19 is a hymn to spiritual and heartfelt purity, immaculateness and innocence, and the need to build a wondrous city in the soul. Here we have a purely Baroque theme of the battle in an individual of natural and unnatural sources, one that was rendered by a number of poets of the time.

And lastly, the third group of ten songs propounds a series of new ideas. The first is the search for happiness in the world (song 21), the next the need to seek eternal values (song 22). Song 23 illuminates the attitude toward time and its use, the next returns to the theme of spiritual peace and the battle with sorrow (song 24). Three panegyrics to spiritual individuals—N. Yakubovych, I.

Kozlovych, and I. Mytkevych—promote the ideas that a worthy person in a worthy position is joy to the world and the nation (songs 25-27). Song 28 has an authorial explanatory note: "About the mysterious and eternal joy inside of God-loving hearts," and it witnesses that happiness mostly depends on itself. And once again Skovoroda repeats the idea of life being like a stormy sea, and the desire of an individual to be saved (song 29). The final summary song combines all the previous themes: time, sorrow, goodness, a life in God, satisfaction through small things and affirmation that death is not "loss," but peace, i.e., a return to the first theme—death.

The discussion here cannot lead to the conclusion that since Skovoroda was traditional in his system of poetics, that he likewise traditionally selected themes. Baroque Ukrainian poetry cultivated all the above-listed themes and motifs in different ways and at different times. The poet does not emerge from beyond his thematic circle even in other poems that were not included in the collection. The difference and even the originality of Skovoroda is in the fact that he often combined known motifs, borrowed from literary sources, especially works of antiquity, from the Bible, from distant Ukrainian poetic works, into his own system of thinking. That is, he gave his poetry the power of a universal vision of the world and humankind, touching on the most cardinal problems of human existence and the make-up of the world. This kind of thematic borrowing is one of the most characteristic features of Baroque poetics. When you summarize it all, Skovoroda makes two main pronouncements: one about the art of living in this world to remain spiritually pure in it, and another about the art of dying. These, of course, were not Skovoroda's own ideas. Christianity propounded them as well as all of the world's Baroque literature. It is as though Skovoroda is recapitulating the experience of the design of the world that existed before him, and applies this experience concretely to his personal "I," i.e., he drew this experience close, directly to the existence of a person, and on this basis formulated his ethical and moral teachings, the science of living in a difficult and complex world. He not only thought and tried to understand the world, he wanted to maintain the purity of his personal "I" in it, and at the same time to help others accomplish this. To this end recall his wonderful aphorism: "Unearth in yourself a well for the water that wets your homestead and your neighbor's."

Skovoroda's *Kharkiv Fables*,[8] just as the *Garden of Divine Songs*, comprise 30 individual works. They were written in the 1760s-1770s. The first 15 were written around 1769, the remainder completed in the village of Babai. At that time the poet philosopher has already left his pedagogical activities, and already has written a series of philosophical dialogues: "Narcissus, Know Thyself," "Askhan, a Book about Knowing Thyself," "Two Conversations, Spoken by Zion," "A Dialogue or Conversation about the Ancient World," "A Conversation of Five Travelers about True Happiness in Life." In these, in fact, Skovoroda had formulated his circle of thought. That is why it was possible for him to write a book of fables, for the thinker in this way popularized and translated into the language of parables his thoughts and views on the world. As in the *Garden of Divine Songs*, Skovoroda in his fables fixes a triangle for his readers: evil, good, and a person at a crossroads, in the fables most often in a beast's mask, and that person must

---

8 For a collection of Skovoroda's fables see: Gregory S. Skovoroda, *Fables and Aphorisms*, Trans. Dan B. Chopyk (New York: Peter Lang, 1990).

choose the straight or crooked path. In the fables we see nearly all the ideas that he worked out in his philosophical treatises.

Legends and anecdotes have been composed about Skovoroda, but all those who met him laud that meeting. With a staff in his hand, with a flute and a bag of books, he walked the roads of Ukraine, and the power of his spirit and his personal example was such that people could not help but feel that this man, though, perhaps, a bit strange in their eyes, with his chimerical stoicism, with his refusal to eat meat or fish, was a special person. It was not for nothing that he decreed that on his grave the following epitaph should be inscribed: "The world tried to catch him, but never did." In fact the world really did try to catch him. According to the requirements of the time, instructors of the collegia and academies had to be monks. When Skovoroda entered the pedagogy department of the Kharkiv Collegium, Bishop I. Mytkevych, by and large well disposed to Skovoroda, ordered abbot H. Yakubovych to convince the thinker to enter the monastic order. But in being a monk, would he be able to live and think freely? He would then be forced to become a wheel in the spiritual mechanism, which by his reckoning, bode no future for him. His mission was to become a small cog that works for the great universal concern. He spoke of this in his fable: "The Wheels of the Clock":

"Tell me," one wheel of the clock machinery asked of another, "Why aren't you turning in the opposite direction from us?"

The other answered: "That's how my master made me, so I don't just get in the way, but even help, so that your clock should have a single path along the circle of the sun."

And he completed the fable about himself with the following moral of the tale: "People with various inclinations have different life paths. However, all of them have a single goal: honesty, harmony, love."

So, Skovoroda could not enjoy the pleasures in this world that demanded that all the wheels turn only in one direction. This not only contradicted his views, but also failed to give him the opportunity to actualize one of the most basic ideas of his own life: to live the way he taught. He wanted to live this way, so that these three eternal truths would prevail: honesty, harmony and love.

One cannot say that contemporaries approached Skovoroda negatively. In looking over the facts of his life, it is not difficult to note that people wanted to take care of him in many places. The landowner Tomara took him to his own home where he taught almost by being compelled. They suggest that he take the ordinary path—to acquire rank and merit, and they acted this way not out of bad intentions, but rather naively believed that this person with his intelligence and talents would find it easy to achieve the highest echelons of the church hierarchy. In fact, the thinker's life turned out just as he wished: it had much bitterness and many unpleasantries, poverty and difficulties, but, as he himself said: "The nature of beauty is such that the more stumbling blocks you come across on your path, the more it allures, to the example of that most noble and hardest of metals, which, the more it's polished, the more beautifully it shines."[9]

He lived as he knew how. Independent, selfish, even proud, a bit strange, wretchedly, but wisely. He aroused conscience in others and taught. "What is life?" He asked. "It is wandering. I lay out the road for me, without knowing where to go, or why. And always

---

9   *Sad pisen'* (Kyiv, 1983), 169.

I wander between the unhappy steppes, prickly bushes, mountainous crevasses — and there's a storm over your head with nowhere to hide from it. But, finishing this somewhat unhappy tirade, he says "take courage!" Thus he walked the roads of Ukraine, carrying the tested purity of his own thoughts, his intelligence and restlessness, his lesson of goodness.

In the 1770s and 1780s he wrote the remainder of his philosophical works: "The Alphabet of the World, or a Friendly Conversation about the Spiritual World," "The Alcibiadiaisian Icon," "Lot's Wife," "The Struggle of Archangel Michael with Satan," "The Altercation of the Demon with Varsava," two parables, "Grateful Herodias" and "The Lowly Skylark," and "The Serpent's Flood." Thus he was 50-60 years old when his main philosophical works were written.

His first worry was to erect his house not on sand, but on stone. Therefore, the philosophical heritage of not only the ancient world and western European thinkers, but even of his native Ukrainian people, became his rock. This is not a gratuitous thesis: the first Ukrainian thinker from the time of Kyivan Rus appropriated the traditions of Neo-Platonism, which favored affirmation of the pantheistic imagination, when God and nature were considered identical concepts. This supported the fact that the ancestors of Ukrainians at that time still had not abandoned their naturistic pantheism that they professed, since they were pagans. But on the Ukrainian land Christianity took root, entering into a compromise with a pagan worldview for the real masses of people. This pre-humanistic worldview created the preconditions for the appropriation of Renaissance ideas in 16th century Ukraine, therefore Latin Renaissance poetry flowered.

It is interesting that we find the bases for Skovoroda's thinking, as scholars have noted, in the abovementioned Ivan Vysensky, and especially in one of the most ancient Ukrainian philosophers from the first half of the 17th century—Kyrylo Trankvilion-Stavrovetsky, the author of *The Mirror of Theology* (1618) and *The Teaching Gospel* (1619). He also led a wandering life and was a poet (*The Pearl of Great Value*), and in the same way as Skovoroda, promoted the cult of reason, writing a poetic hymn to it "On Supreme Wisdom." But with his philosophical works he transgressed the boundaries of Christian dogma, thereby provoking condemnations, which led to the burning of his books. Skovoroda's teachers—Mytrofan Dovhalevsky ("The main thing in life is reason, and all the rest perishes without trace") and Georgy Konysky ("In praise of logic")—also penned hymns to reason. Therefore, for Skovoroda, God is universal reason, eternity, fate, that power that sets the entire universe into motion, like a clock mechanism, the creator of harmony in the world, the mechanism of being. God and nature are precisely one and the same. This universal reason created the world, which is divided from one perspective into matter and form, and from another into the macrocosm (the great world) and the microcosm (the small world). The macrocosm is nature, the cosmos, that also is composed of form and matter, and the microcosm—an individual and the world of symbols (the Bible) that is the shadow of universal reason. A person, as an element of the microcosm, has in himself the flesh and spirit. The flesh is visible, mutable, the sins and passions, the feral in us, while the spirit is the invisible, the immutable that brings an individual peace, eternal freedom and thought. Upon death, the individual enters his origin—nothingness, that is, the origin and end are one and the same. To this point recall that the *Garden of Divine Songs* begins and ends with the thought of death.

The decisive aspect of Skovoroda's philosophy, as well as his predecessors, is the special attention he gives to the individual as well as to the living world. The individual, he noted, is born as an animal, he has to be born a second time spiritually. And everyone born in this world is a wanderer ("Like I was born, even now I'm a traveler!"). An individual, figuratively speaking, is a blind person, who must find his pupils in order to recover his sight (Skovoroda's parable of the blind and legless man). The beginning of that recovery of sight is in reconciliation with one's spirit, and when irreconcilability occurs, the individual then enters into an incommensurable state, he takes on an uncomforting obligation, and through this comes to understand sorrow, longing, and boredom (the fable of the cats from "The Alphabet of the World"). From here one of Skovoroda's great ideas flows: about the affinity for work, that is this affinity entering into harmony with nature. Woe to him, who, born for great deeds, is forced to amble about in small circles, but it is society's woe when someone born to live in small circles, takes high positions. So that this should not occur, one needs to know himself, to differentiate good from evil, for good and evil live in the same individual. There is no hell or heaven outside of an individual, they are within him, for in each individual a merciless battle of the principles of darkness and light is waged. Again, an individual, just like a traveler, has several roads: real and false ones. On this basis the thinker constructs his teachings about happiness. In chasing after it an individual hurriedly traverses the earth's sphere, seeking it beyond the seas, in foreign lands, forgetting that you need to seek happiness not outside of yourself, but within, in self-perfection, in conscience, in good reason that will give the individual the ability to become spiritual, and at the same time a chosen being of a higher order. He teaches that one must understand the world not by the shell, but by the yolk." "Collect inside you these thoughts," he wrote, "and inside yourself seek true blessings." And further on: "You must have time for everything, place and measure, for the next cheerfully illuminated day is the fruit of yesterday." From this one, another Skovorodian idea emerges, which he took from Epicurus and developed further: what is necessary is easy, and the unnecessary difficult, that is, whatever you have a disposition toward, you eagerly do with ease, but something to be done that is unseemly is difficult and done unwillingly. An individual, divided by free will, is capable of coming to the creation of a social formation—the unification of such enlightened people can occur in "the mountainous republic." However, Skovoroda does not differentiate between people by their social status, origin, or place in society, or, figuratively speaking, by their clothing, but by the measure of their spiritual elevation, their closeness to the ideal of an individual. Such a person is a chosen one and is counterposed to the throng and to the person of the throng, who as one has not yet abandoned his feral origin. The life of a person is a movement away from the feral (body) to the spiritual; the traveling companion of such a person must be poverty and simplicity.

Thus all of Skovoroda's works are a profoundly conceived whole. The thinker, through his philosophical treatises on one level, through his poems-songs on another, and through his fables and parables on a third, along with the assistance of oral sermons, taught those who wanted to learn, and was a teacher in the broad sense of the word. He went where he was welcome, where his sagacious word was needed. "Love emerges from love," he wrote, "when I want to be loved, I first love." And he also wrote: "Everything passes, but love remains after everything."[10]

One other topic should be examined to comprehend the phenomenon of Skovoroda adequately—that is the language of his writings, for he wrote in a complicated, chimerical language, one even closer to Russian than Ukrainian. This is a not particularly simple question and in order to resolve it, one must take a brief historical excursion.

The language of the Eastern or Byzantine Rite, before it was called Orthodox, was invented by the Slavic enlighteners Cyril and Methodius in the 9th century AD and called Old Church Slavic. That written and primarily liturgical language, fusing with the local, i.e., Ukrainian, became the literary language of Kyivan Rus. If you take the chronicle *Tale of Bygone Years* or *The Lay of Ihor's Campaign*, it is not difficult to note that one finds many Ukrainian words and even verbal constructions, but the basis for that language was Old Church Slavic. Later in the Great Lithuanian Principality, one additional variant of this language appeared, constructed on the basis of Old Church Slavic with elements of the Ukrainian and the Belarusian languages. Later that bookish language (this occurred in the 16th century) divided into bookish Ukrainian and bookish Belarusian. Bookish Ukrainian had become formed completely at the end of the 16th century and existed in Ukraine along with other literary languages —Polish and Latin, however, it appropriated elements of these other languages. Such a hybrid language was in use approximately until the middle of the 18th

---

10   *Sad pisen'*, 165, 169.

century, after which in Ukraine the Russian language was forcibly introduced in schools. At that time Latin was still used, but the use of Polish in Eastern, Left Bank Ukraine ended. We see this in Skovoroda's writings. From the beginning of the 18th century a different tendency can be noted: a return to the Old Church Slavic language, which was replete to a certain degree with Ukrainianisms, and called "Slavic." Most dramatic works that were staged at the Kyiv Academy were written in it, the chronicle of Hryhory Hrabyanka, and a series of poems (Ivan Maksymovych wrote in this language exclusively). Bookish Ukrainian existed parallel with Slavic, with chronicles (Samiylo Velychko), poems, and other works written in it. With the introduction of the foundations of the Russian language forcibly introduced into schools, there was created a unique bookish hybrid language that might be called "made close to Russian." That is, this was already the Russian language with a certain amount of Ukrainianisms. A number of authors wrote in that language: Hnat Maksymovych, the monk Yakiv, Semen Dilovych, the anonymous author of *The History of the Rus People*, Irynei Falkivsky, Hryhory Skovoroda, and others. But Skovoroda's language has unique properties: one can differentiate various layers in it. The poetry, besides that in Latin, is written in bookish Ukrainian, in Slavic, in a Ukrainianized language, and in a Russianized language. The fables and philosophical works are written in a Russianized language. Why did Skovoroda do this? Primarily, because this was the language of the schools of his time, the language of educated society. The thinker addressed that society in the language in which it was taught. But the time-honored tradition of the bookish Ukrainian language did not disappear, and his spoken Ukrainian influenced his written Russian, just as many

Ukrainian words, phraseology, sayings, proverbs, and Church Slavonicisms entered into the written language of his contemporaries. The thinker himself had a great aptitude for languages: he knew ancient Greek and Latin, quotes entire sentences and words in German, perhaps knew French, and certainly knew ancient Hebrew. At the beginning of the parable "Grateful Herodias," Skovoroda presents the greeting by Pishek in an entire series of languages. This is a deeply rooted Ukrainian tradition of literary multilinguality. It has always been considered that the more languages an individual knows, the more educated he is. By making use of various languages, he projects greater scholarly erudition. The Ukrainian language and folk language was that of song, of folk versification, of *intermedia* to dramas, that is, folk scenarizations. Only from the activities of the Pochaiv cultural circle in the West and Ivan Kotlyarevsky in Eastern Ukraine, did language acquire the status of a viable literary language. Thus Skovoroda in this plan linguistically was just a child of his time. Skovoroda was not a national writer per se. He often spoke with contempt of simpletons, of the throng, of a person of low development. The thinker, thus, wrote for the educated stratum of his people and often expressed the elite nature of his thinking. The contradictions of wealth and the apologia for poverty did not mean that he looked at the common people as though they were a carrier of higher wisdom. The language Skovoroda used in his works is an incontrovertible fact that proves the philosopher addressed his teachings not to the simple people, but rather to the educated. It is quite another issue that the common people appropriated his works, particularly his songs that they sang. But it is quite interesting that folk singers Ukrainianized the texts of the songs, that is, the songs were clothed in the national vernacular Ukrainian language and continued to live on, while maintaining the name of Skovoroda's psalms. In fact, the late romantics Panteileimon Kulish and Taras Shevchenko reproached Skovoroda most for his language, for they reasoned that Ukrainian literature could not take that path. In the end, not long after Skovoroda's death in 1794, Ukrainians had to choose whether to take the path of Russian (taken by Vasyl Kapnist, Nikolai Gogol (Mykola Hohol in Ukrainian), Vasyl Narezhny, Orest Somov, and a whole series of other writers), or both simultaneously (Kulish, Mykola Kostomarov, Hryhory Kvitka-Osnovianenko, Evhen Hrebinka, Marko Vovchok, Taras Schevchenko), or just the Ukrainian. But Ukrainian literati began to write exclusively in Ukrainian only in the second half of the 19th century (Ivan Nechui-Levytsky, Panas Myrny). Even the great Ukrainian writer Ivan Franko used Polish and German as his literary languages at the turn of the century.

Regardless, Hryhory Skovoroda was a great teacher of his people. The power of his reason has become more widespread over time, for he could see through the world and a person. He spoke to his contemporaries the honest, deliberate and sagacious word, and that word was heard not only by his contemporaries, but also by many generations to come.

> – Valery Shevchuk, Kyiv, Ukraine
> *Translated from the Ukrainian*
> *by Michael M. Naydan with minor*
> *abridgments from the original*
> *typescript.*

The Garden of Divine Songs[11]

Blossoming from the seeds of the Holy Bible

---

[11] The Ukrainian word "Sad," which I translate here as "garden," may also be translated as "orchard."

FIRST SONG

Composed in 1757 according to this virtue:
"Blessed are the undefiled in the way, who walk in the law of the Lord."[12]

People dread descending to the grave to decay,
So that afterward they do not partake [in turn]
Of the place where eternal fire burns;
But death is sacred, our wicked life ends,
Transfiguring our wicked strife into peace.
                              O, this sacred death!

He who has a conscience clear not even
                        a blazing Perun does fear![13]
He does not burn in hellfire['s tears],
He lives the life of paradise.
O, sin gives birth to death! It brings a living death,
From death comes hell; hunger burns the soul.
                              O, this savage death!

---

12   Psalms 118(119):1-2. I will primarily be quoting from the King James version of the Bible to mimic the more archaic sound of Skovoroda's 18-th century poetry, though when the text of that varies from Skovoroda's version, I will emend and note those instances to make them closer to Skovoroda's actual quotations. The numbering of the Psalms in the Slavic Bible translated from the Septuagint Greek differs from English Bibles translated from the Hebrew. I will give the Slavic Bible's number first and the English Bible's number in parentheses in further instances of quotations from the Book of Psalms.

13   Perun was the chief ancient Slavic god, the god of thunder and equivalent to Zeus.

Blessed, O blessed is he from the cradle
Who has dedicated himself to Christ,
Day and night he reflects in His word,
Having accepted the good yoke and light burden,
He who becomes inured to this, who makes it habit['s trait].
                        O, this holy fate!

He who has partaken of this sweetness can
Never plummet into the profane, no!
In nakedness, in misfortune he will not yearn;

Neither fire nor sword will separate him [firm];
Pleasure all the more leads him astray.
                It does not lay upon his heart.
Except for him, who allows it to do so [in part].
                He let us come to understand costly temptation.

Christ, my life, you died for me!
I should have given You my early years,
I give You all the rest!
Cleanse the stone of my heart. Kindle your flame in it.
And bring death to the passions and evil pleasures,
                I live for you my light [my treasure].

And when I arise from my sins, when I adorn the heavenly flesh,
You will abide in me, and I will settle in you,
I will be sated by that sweetness,
Deliberating with you, taking counsel [here],
Like the sunset, like the rising sun.
                O! This is an age of golden years!

1757

                        The End.

SECOND SONG

From this seed:
"and whatsoever thou shalt bind
on earth shall be bound in heaven."[14]

Leave soon, o spirit of mine, all earthly places!
Ascend, my spirit, onto the mountains where Holy truth dwells,
Where peace and silence eternally reign,
Where the land glows, where the light is beyond reach.

Leave your earthly sorrows![15] and the vanity of worldly things!
Be pure, at least for a short time, so you can fly upward,
Where the Lord of Jacob dwells, where unfading Sunset abides,
Where all the Angelic hosts always see his face [to guide].[16]

These are the waters of Siloam![17]
                                        Wash away the filth from your eyes,
Wash all the parts of your body to fly to the heavens [up high],
For with an impure heart one cannot see the Lord,
And an earthbound person cannot fly to those places [adored].

---

14   Matthew 16:19.

15   This line echoes the words of the Cherubic Hymn of the Divine Liturgy of St. John Chrysostom. In Old Church Slavic the relevant line is: "Vsiakoe nyne zhiteiskoe otlozhim popechenie" (Let us now set aside our earthy worries). In vernacular Ukrainian and Russian the last word would be "pechal'," which is precisely the world found in Skovoroda's original.

16   From Matthew 18:10. "Take heed that ye despise not one of these little ones; for I say unto you, That in heaven their angels do always behold the face of my Father which is in heaven." (KJV).

17   The waters of Siloam are where Christ instructed a blind man to bathe his eyes with mud. The man was rewarded with the gift of sight. See Paul 9: 7-11.

Our soul cannot be content with the carnal [medium],
It burns only with the heavenly to sate tedium,
The way a stream swiftly flows to the sea,
        the way steel jumps at a magnet,
A flame flickers up to mountains,
          so our spirit bursts through for a glimpse of the Lord.

Abandon this entire befouled world.
                   It is veritably a dark hell[to pity].
Let the foul black enemy fly away.
                  You rise onto the mountain city
And, walking along the earth, settle in the heavens,
The way Paul teaches you with his words so pure.

Rush to eternal happiness from here with wings so wise,
You will restore your joy there like
                 a swift-winged eagle [that flies].
O, thrice-holy one! The word is more exalted than all!
Who can grasp this with their mind?
             Besides one descended from heaven.

                           The End.

THIRD SONG

From this seed:
"Let the earth bring forth grass, the herb yielding seed."[18] That is: "and your bones shall flourish like an herb."[19]

*

Beloved spring, ah, you've come!
      Ferocious winter, ah, you've gone!
Already the gardens have bloomed and brought the nightingales.

Ah, you, sadness, be gone from here!
      Don't bespoil the beautiful villages.
Run to the swamps, to underworld gates!

Run away, off to hell! Paradise and the garden are not for you.
My soul has blossomed and brought joys.

Happy is he who without worldly
      comforts has conquered mortal sin.
His soul is the city of God, his soul is God's garden [within].

This garden always brings forth flowers,
      it always brings forth fruit,
In the spring it always blooms, and its leaves never fall.

Lord! Thou art my city! Lord, Thou art my garden!
Innocence for me is the flowers, love
      and peace — the fruits [of the hour].

---

18 Genesis 1:11.
19 Isaiah 66:14.

My soul is a willow, and you the water for it.
Nourish me in this water, comfort me in distress.

I fear nothing [known]; I fear just sins alone.
Inside me kill all manner of sin:
                        this is the key to my comfort within!

FOURTH SONG

For the Birth of Christ from this seed:
"The Lord is with us! Understand, people. 20" That is:
"God has anointed us in his Spirit."[21] "God hath sent
forth the Spirit of his Son into your hearts."[22]

Angels descend. Come closer to the earth,
For the Lord maker of the ages lives with men [upon his birth].
   Arise ye all higher in the choir, congregation?
   Rejoice! For the Lord is with us [to inspire].[23]

Behold the time is coming to pass!
                 Behold the Son has been sent [at last]!
The time has come to a close! God is sending us His Son.
   The day is nigh. The Virgin giving birth.
   Rejoice! For the Lord is with us.

Promised by the prophets, by the Father's heralds[' appeal],
In end times it will be resolved. The New Testament's seal.
   The spirit of freedom is awakening in us,
   Rejoice! For the Lord is with us.

---

20   From the Christmas Vesper service: http://www.pastoral.org.ua/?p=254.

21   Paraphrase of 2 Corinthians 21-22. I have translated directly from Skovoroda's original here. The KJV reads: "Now he which stablisheth us with you in Christ, and hath anointed us, is God; Who hath also sealed us, and given the earnest of the Spirit in our hearts."

22   From the First Epistle of Paul to the Galatians 4:6.

23   The refrain is repeatedly sung in the Byzantine Orthodox Christmas vesper service.

O stone of Daniel! The flame of the burning bush!
Uncut you will fall away! Fire will not ignite hay [from the brush]!
   This is our stone! This is our flame!
   Rejoice! For the Lord is with us [in name].

O, Grace, our new intercessor, thrive!
Thrive and you will arise, you will burn away foes [alive].
   And all existence, seen redeemed,
   All rejoice, for the Lord is with us.

For Thee who is born, for our Blessed Guest,
We open our hearts, calling Thee into our spiritual home [blessed],
   Singing a song, proclaiming,
   Rejoicing, for the Lord is with us.

The End.

FIFTH SONG

To the Birth of Christ. From this seed:
"And she brought forth her firstborn son, and wrapped
him in swaddling clothes, and laid him in a manger."[24]

Mystery so strange and glorious!
A manger instead of the heavens!
The Virgin at the head of the cherubim [victorious],
The throne most high today.
And He lies entirely in the crèche,
Which is too small
   For the heaven of heavens.

O blessed are those eyes!
That behold this mystery.
Those whom a star at wicked worldly
Midnight led to the Lord.
The angelic mind sees this mystery,
But a flesh and blood man loathes it,
   Because everyone like him wants to rebel.

With our ever-burning heart we revere
This heavenly secret,
And though like cattle incapable of words
We eat the straw beneath Christ.
Until, growing up into a perfect
Man, we can partake of blessed
   God Himself.

                                                The End.

---

24   Luke 2:7.

SIXTH SONG

At the end of this seed:
"And the serpent cast out of his mouth water as a flood after the woman, that he might cause her to be carried away by the flood."[25] "But God shall wound the head of his enemies."[26]

Attend the heaven and earth! Be in awe today.
Sea, with all your abysses, move in harmony.
And you, swift-flowing Jordan, return.
John, come quickly to baptize Christ!

Beautiful forests, open up your paths.
Let John the forerunner proceed to Christ.
Earthly peoples, exult with us in unison.
Angelic choirs, everyone in heaven rejoice.

The Savior descended upon the Jordan, stood in its depths,
And the Holy Spirit in the form of a dove descended upon Him.
This is my beloved Son, the Father from the clouds proclaimed:
This Messiah will renew all creation.

Bless the streams for us. Cleave the Serpent's head.tear off
Christ, give us the dew and glory of your spirit,
And the Serpent will not swallow us.
                        And all of us from the earthly vale
Will lie down to rest in your paradise [without fail].

                                                    The End.

---

25   Revelations 12: 15.
26   Psalms 68: 21. This is Psalm 67: 22 in Slavic bibles.

SEVENTH SONG

For the Resurrection of Christ. From this seed:
"Then the eleven disciples went away into Galilee,
into a mountain where Jesus had appointed them."[27]

Who can separate me from your love?
Can I grow weary of this mystical flame? strange, eerie
May the whole world be gone!
I will live in you,
                      O Jesus!

Lead me with you on the mountain path to the cross.
I am happy to live above the mountain.
                I will cast away the vale's dust.
Your death is life for me,
Your bile is like sweets for me,
                      O Jesus!

Your grave sores are – my sign,
Your thorny crown to me – glory's grace [divine],
This Cross that you bear
Is praise and honor for me,
                      O Jesus!

If a grain of wheat were to rot in the fields.
If the outside is not alive, a new fruit will bloom inside.
Into a single old ear of wheat
In the coming summer time of heat [acute]
                the hundred-year-old grain will bear fruit.

---

[27]   Matthew 28:16.

Crucify my body, nail it to the cross.
Let me not be whole without so I can be reborn within.
Let my external self wither away!
And a new inner self blossom [today].
                      This is a living death.

O my new Adam! O most beautiful Son!
O universal shame! O rebellions of Athens!
Underneath your rebellion is – the light!
Underneath death — eternal life [in sight].
                      Until the shroud is dark!

                                    The End.

EIGHTH SONG

For the Resurrection of Christ. From this seed:
"O! O! Flee to the mountains!"[28] "O sleeper? arise."[29]
"The Lord will give peace on this mountain."[30]

Death-dealing wounds have covered me;
Intolerable hellish woes have surrounded me;
Fear and darkness have come upon me. O, ferocious hour!
                The hour of evil!

The stiff thorn of sickness bangs into my bowels!
My soul is sorrowful,
                sorrowful even toward death['s power].
Ah, who will deliver me from this hour?
                Who will make me whole again?

The swift African deer suffers this way.
It rushes to the mountains swifter than birds to drink.
But thirst burns inside, sated with a serpent soaked, drenched
                And all manner of venom [spent].

I will quicken my pace in rushing to Golgotha['s face].
There my healer lies hanging between two thieves.

---

28   Zechariah 14:5. Skovoroda's version is slightly at variance with the King James Version and other Slavic Bibles I have consulted including the OCS version. I have opted for a literal translation of the original here, which Skovoroda may be paraphrasing or quoting inexactly. The KJV reads: "And ye shall flee to the valley of the mountains."

29   Jonah 1:6.

30   Isaiah 25:10. I have given the literal translation from the original here. The KJV reads: "For in this mountain shall the hand of the Lord rest."

Behold John sobbing at the cross [for his loss]!
>> He kisses the cross.

O, Jesus! My consolation!
Are you still alive here? A martyr's elation!
In this passion give me the cure of salvation.
>> Do not let me ever fall.

>> The End.

NINTH SONG

To the Holy Spirit. From this:
"Thy spirit is good; lead me into the land of uprightness."[31] "Go to, let us go down, and there confound their language, that they may not understand one another's speech."[32]

*Each head has its own reason.cognizance?
Each heart its own love['s season],
Yet not all those alive have the same thought:
One prefers sheep, another goats.
Thus freedom for me alone is testy,
And a sorrow-free, truly simple path.
Behold my chief measure in life.
My entire circle will end here.

You, most holy Lord and creator of the ages,
Affirm what you yourself created [on your pages].
With you all can lead to a blessed end
The way steel attracted to a magnet bends.
But my eye sees falsely,
You, Heavenly Father, teach me here.
You see the people, from sitting on high,
Such countless different minds [passing by].

He who goes east into the sunset landsevening lands
Floats along seeking happiness in full sail,
Another sees paradise in the midnight land,north
A third finds his path to the south [first hand].

---

31   Psalm 142(143): 10.

32   Genesis 11:7.

One says: someone is reaping there!
Another argues that someone is shearing.cutting
And a third: utters "the cart has five wheels."
Tell us: what manner of devil cleaves our thoughts into dust?

                                                      The End.

TENTH SONG

From this seed:
"Blessed is the man who dies in wisdom and who studies in the temple."[33]

Every city has its customs and laws.
Every head has its own mind.
Every heart has its own love.
Every palate has its own taste.
But for me there is only one thought in this world.
Just one thing never leaves my mind.

For rituals Pyotr scrubs every corner for the masters.
Fedka the merchant always lies when he's measuring.
One builds his home in a new style.
One, if you will, traffics in interest, be sure to verify!
But for me there is only one thought in this world.
Just one thing never leaves my mind.

One constantly strikes the ground.
A stranger pastures cattle.
They ready dogs for the hunt.
The house of some bustles from guests like a tavern.
But for me there is only one thought in this world,
Just one thing never leaves my mind.

---

33 From the apocryphal Ecclesiasticus, or the Wisdom of Jesus Son of Sirach. Skovoroda's quotation echoes Sirach 1:13: "Whoso feareth the Lord, it shall go well with him at the last, and he shall find favour in the day of his death." (KJV).

  A jurist makes laws in his own tone,
A student's head aches from disputes.
Venus' Cupid occupies the mind of some.
Everyone's own folly torments his head.
But for me there is a single thought in this world,
Just one thing never leaves my mind.

  O terrifying death! O threatening scythe!
You won't even spare the hair on a king's head.
You won't look whether it's a peasant or king [dead],
You devour the way a fire devours straw.
Who can scorn its sharp steel [maw]
Only one whose conscience is crystal clear.

ELEVENTH SONG

To this end:
"Deep calleth unto deep."[34] That is: "But his will is in the law of the Lord."[35] "I would give you the water of life,"[36] will to your will, and my abyss to your abyss.[37]

You cannot cover the ocean's abyss with a handful of dust.
You cannot cool a fire with a meager droplet.
Will an eagle be able to soar in a dark cave?
For did he fly from here into the heavenly lands?
    And the spirit will not be sated by the flesh.

The spirit in man is an abyss,
                  wider than all the waters and heavens.
You will not sate for eternity
                  what captivates the vision of your eyes.
From here comes tedium. It creaks inside, languor, sorrow.
From here comes the lack of satiety. From a droplet
                  the heat becomes worse.
    Know! Spirit will not be sated by the flesh.

---

34   Psalms (41)42:7.

35   Psalms 1:2. The Russian Synodal and OCS versions of the Bible use the word "volya" (meaning "freedom" or "will") instead of "delight," which is found in the KJV. Thus I have used "will" here to better match Skovoroda's original.

36   John 4:10.

37   Note 70 in the Ushkalov Skovoroda edition indicates that this comprises Skovoroda's commentary on the passage from John (p. 97).

O race of the flesh! Louts! How long will you be heavyhearted?
Raise the eyelids of the heart! Gaze upon the firmament.
Why do you not seek to know what is called God?
Why do you not try to comprehend so that you can see Him?
    The abyss suddenly calls the abyss.

                                                         The End.

TWELFTH SONG

From this seed:
"Blessed are the poor in spirit."[38] That is: "The wisdom of a learned man cometh by opportunity of leisure: and he that hath little business shall become wise."[39]
"to bring to nought things that are."[40]

1. I'll not go to the moneyed city.
                         I'll live in the fields.
   I'll pass through my life where time quietly rushes on.
   O oak grove! O green grove! O dear mother of mine!
   In you life is joyful. In you there is peace and quiet.

2. Glorious towering cities drive you to the sea of sorrows.
   Beautiful gates, so wide – lead to bitter captivity.
   O oak grove!.. O green grove! And so forth.

3. I do not want to travel to the sea, nor do I desire fine clothes.
   Beneath them grief is concealed, sorrows, fear, and rebellion.
   O oak grove!.. And so forth.

4. I don't yearn to capture cities to the beat of drums,
   I don't yearn to frighten petty officials
                         with high office.
   O oak grove!.. And so forth.

---

[38]   Matthew 5:3.
[39]   Sirach 38:24.
[40]   Corinthians 1:28.

5. I don't want any new lessons other than a sound mind.
   Other than Christ's wisdom, whose thought is sweet.
   O oak grove!.. And so forth.

6. I wish for nothing but bread and water.
   Poverty is my friend, we have been kin for a long time.
   O oak grove!.. And so forth.

7. Peace and holy freedom – from all corporeal estates.
   Besides the heavenly eternities, life alone is sacred for me.
   O oak grove!.. And so forth.

8. And if in addition to these pleasures I am victorious over sin,
   Then I do not know whether
                   anything could be better than these comforts.
   O oak grove!.. And so forth.

9. Greetings, my cherished peacefulness!
                   Eternally you will be mine.
   It is good for me to be with you:
                   be mine forever and I will be yours.
   O oak grove! O freedom! In you I began to grow wise,
   My nature is for you, in you I want to die.

                                                    The End.

THIRTEENTH SONG

From this:
"Wherefore come out from among them..."[41] *That is:*
"Go ye into the village over against you."[42] *"There thy mother brought thee forth."*[43]

O fields! Fields of green!
Fields covered with flowers!
O the valleys! The ravines!
Round mounds! The hillocks!hillocks?

O you, pure streams of water!
O you, grass covered shores!
O your hair! Curly-haired forests!

A skylark amid fields,
A nightingale among gardens.
One flying upward chirps, another whistles on branches.

And when the day is breaking,
All manner of birds whistle.
The air diffused by music rustles all around.

Right when the sun appears,
A shepherd drives his sheep [to shear].
And on his flute imparts a trembling trill.

---

41   2 Corinthians 6:17.
42   Luke 19:30.
43   Songs of Solomon 8:5.

Be gone, weighty thoughts!
Swarming cities.
I will die in just such a place with just a piece of bread.

The End.

FOURTEENTH SONG

An ancient Little Russian[44] song about vanity and worldly flattery._
According to this virtue:
"I will stand upon my watch, and set me upon a stone."[45]
Revised in 1782.

1.
What of glory today?
      Fix your eyes on bedlam in this hour!
O Israel! Hydras of the beast,
      You need to understand
           The great scope of it.

2.
Today the scepter and mace.
      In waking the next morning glory is base.
The heart is pierced through.
      Hands and feet are bound [too].
           How do you elude the net.

3.
Today drunken freedom bounds,
      In waking the next morning, fate is futile [all around].

---

44   The condescending and now pejorative name that Russians had for Ukraine and Ukrainians from tsarist times. Skovoroda had no pejorative connotations when he uses the appellation in his writings.

45   Habbakuk 2:1. The Synodal Russian Bible has "na bashne" (a tower), while the KJV has "the tower." Skovoroda seems to be quoting from the Old Church Slavic Bible, which has "a stone" (na kamen').

O, Israel! Belly of the beast,
> Where does your aim and excess lead you [to creep]?
>> You need to see deeper.

4.
The flattering Siren of the sea!
> With the sweet voice of charm.
A poor soul on his way
> Seeks repose forever [in harm],
>> Without ever reaching the shore.

5.
Flesh! The world! O insatiable hell!
> All is poison for you, you are poison to all!
Day and night your jaws gape.
> Without even a glance you will swallow all.
>> Who can elude the net?

6.
Behold the abyss engulfs everyone!
> Behold a jaw, consuming all!
O Israel! The great whale beast,[46]
> Behold reason for you, your aim and measure!
>> The flesh will not sate you [ever].

7.
Ah, nimbly set out your sails!
> And the wings of your mind [never fail],
Floating above the stormy sea,
> Lift your eyes upward,
>> And the path will flow truly [forward].

---

46   Skovoroda glosses this, noting that the whale is a symbol of sin.

8.
It is better to live in the desert,
    Locked up in a cave,[47]
To live in deserted places,
    And not hear voices of flattery.

9.
Be a zealous Hercules for me,
    Be a wise Jonah,
Burn the heads of the serpent.
    Out of your whale vomit
        Cast me onto the rock.[48]

        The End.

---

[47] A reference to Lot in Genesis 19:30, who dwelt in a cave with his two daughters as a result of his fear of corruption in the city of Zoar.

[48] "Kefa" (the rock or cliff) is a symbol of the Apostle Peter as Skovoroda points out in a gloss to the image.

FIFTEENTH SONG

For Great Saturday. From this seed:
"And he rested on the seventh day."[49] "That they
should not enter into my rest."[50]

You lie in the grave. You celebrate the Sabbath
Following hard work. After bloody sweat.
The Prince has nothing to do with you [yet],
The Prince of this world who rules over all.
O, these are unheard footsteps!
O, new manner of victory!
O, Son of David!
Son of David, raising Lazarus,
From earthly wisdom to heavenly glory.
Slay the work of the flesh in me!
Allow me to celebrate the Sabbath with Thee.
Let me walk in your footsteps.
Allow a new form of this victory to be.
O Son of David!

The End.

---

49 Genesis 2:2.
50 Psalms 94(95): 11.

SIXTEENTH SONG

According to this virtue:
"I do set my [rain]bow in the cloud." (Genesis 9:13)

Clouds passed. A joyful rainbow shines.
All longing has passed. Our light[51] glimmers [divine].
The heart's merriment is the pure light of radiant sky,
If the gloom and rustling of the world's wind have passed by.

O delightful world! To me you are an ocean, an abyss.
You are gloom, clouds, a whirlwind, longing, woe.
This beautiful rainbow lights up the radiant sky for me,
A heartfelt dove tells me of peace [in its glow].

Farewell, sadness! Farewell, farewell, wicked belly!
I have stood up on my feet, been resurrected from the grave.
O David's branch!
        You are my shore and safe harbor [that saves],[52]
You are a rainbow, life,
    radiant sky for me, light, peace, and an olive branch.

                         The End.

---

51   Skovoroda most often uses the word "mir" to mean "the world." Though "svet" here most often means "light," it also can mean "the world" in Old Church Slavic.

52   Many thanks to William Schmalstieg for initially enlightening me on the meaning of the word "Kifa," an Aramaic nickname for the Apostle Peter. Skovoroda remarks in a note that "Kefa" is the name of a mythical harbor where one could hide from the bustle of the world and dangers at sea.

SEVENTEENTH SONG

"The sea of life that billows in vain,"[53] and so forth.

Seeing the sadness of this life,
Seething like the Red Sea['s strife],
With a whirlwind of sorrows, illness and woes,
I grow weak, terrified, pale [indisposed].
O sadness for those existing in its throes!

I revisited my poor escape quickly,
So as not to bury myself with the Pharoah in the sea.
I run to a quiet harbor [without fail]
And shout out in a lamenting wail,
Lifting my hands high.

O Christ! Do not let me rot in hell!
In your heavenly city let me dwell.
And do not let the world whore,[54] this dark light,
Drag me in its tracks [with all its might]!
O abyss of mercy!

The End.

---

53 According to note #94 of the Ushkalov edition of Skovoroda, this comes from the matins before the Sunday Divine Liturgy, the sixth voice, and the irmos of the sixth song.

54 Skovoroda may be suggesting the Whore of Babylon from Revelations here, though for Skovoroda the world is equivalent to a whore, to one that leads one astray to sin.

EIGTHTEENTH SONG

"God resisteth the proud, but giveth grace unto the humble."[55]

O! Yellow-feathered bird,
Do not build your nest on high.
Build it where the green grass grows,
On the young grass below.
Behold! A hawk above your head
Hanging, it wants to snatch you [dead].
Behold, behold, it lives on your blood!
It's sharpening its claws [with dread].

Atop a hill a sycamore stands,
Shaking its head.
Fierce winds blow,
Breaking the sycamore's arms.
And the willows rustle low,
Dragging me to sleep [below].
A stream is flowing close nearby:
You can see to the very bottom.

Why should I contemplate
That a mother gave birth in a village?
Let the brain of those explode
Who soar up high.
For I will quietly
Spend my cherished lifetime.
All bad things will pass me by,
And I will be a happy man.

The End.

---

55   James 4:6.

NINETEENTH SONG

To this end:
"For we wrestle not against flesh and blood..."[56] *"Thou shalt tread upon the lion and the adder..."*[57] *"And take the [helmet of salvation, and] sword of the Spirit, which is the word of God."*[58]

Ah, you accursed longing! O gnawing sadness [that I feel]!
You've gnawed at me since my youth,
                      like a moth a dress, like rust steel.
O you longing, O you torment! Ferocious torment!
You'll always be with me wherever I go [to lament].
Like a fish in water, you are always beside us.
O you longing! O you torment! Ferocious torment!

You will stab a wicked beast if you take a sharp knife.
But you will not surmount this longing,
                      though your sword is fine.
O you longing! O you torment! Ferocious torment!
The good-hearted WORD pierces those beasts.
It is always ready to enter your thoughts.
O you longing! O you torment! Ferocious torment!

Christ! You are my heavenly sword in the scabbard of our flesh.
Hear our tearful wail. Have mercy on us among these beasts.
O you longing! O you torment! Ferocious torment!
Your sweet-sweet voice will roar for us from high.

---

56   Ephesians 6:12.
57   Psalms (90) 91:13.
58   Ephesians 6:17.

Like lightning you will drive away all the vile beasts.
Be gone, longing! Be gone torment! In smoke and fumes!

> The End.
> *Composed in 1758 in the Pereyaslav*
> *steppes, in the village of Kavrai.*

TWENTIETH SONG

[The city] Named Zoar. In this small but high city Lot carouses with his daughters:[59] "so have we seen in the city of the Lord of hosts, in the city of our God;"[60] "I will liken him unto a wise man, which built his house upon a rock."[61] "Who shall ascend into the hill of the Lord??"[62]

He who is pure of heart and soul
Needs no armor,
Neither does he need a helmet on his neck,
Nor does he need war.
Purity – that is his armor,
And innocence – a diamond wall,
God Himself is his shield, his sword, his helmet[, his all].

O world! World of folly [and things]!
Does your hope lie in kings?
Do you imagine this shore is without slights?
A whirlwind will scatter this dust [with its might].
Purity is – Zoar[63] for you!
And innocence – a heavenly palace!
Fly there! And there repose!

---

59   The story of Lot and his two daughters is in Genesis 19:30-38. The city of Zoar is where Lot dwelled for a time with his daughters after the destruction of Sodom and Gomorrah.

60   Psalms (47) 48:8.

61   Matthew 7:24.

62   Psalms (23) 24:3 as well as a Troparion in the Divine Liturgy for the Feast of the Transfiguration.

63   The biblical city that was spared the fate of Sodom and Gomorrah.

This holy city fears no bombs,
Nor slanderous arrows,
It fears no sly sneers either,grimaces, expressions
It has always stayed whole and never burned.
Purity is the Adamant stone,[64]
And innocence is this holy city.
Fly there! And there repose!

In this city even enemies are loved,
Goodness is offered to them [above].
Others lose their health,
Not only those who have been good to friends.
Where is that so beautiful city?
You yourself are this city,
             after you oust the poison from your soul,
The temple and the city for the Holy Spirit.

                                  The End.

---

64   Reference to the adamant stone appears in Ezekiel 3:9 and Zechariah 7:12.

TWENTY-FIRST SONG

To this end:
"Tell me, O thou whom my soul loveth, where thou feedest, where thou makest thy flock to rest at noon."[65]

Happiness, where do you live? Turtledoves, tell us.
Do you graze the sheep in the fields? Doves, proclaim.announce
    O happiness! Our shining light.
    O happiness! Our beautiful flower [bright].
You are Mother and Home. Appear, reveal yourself.

Happiness! Where do you live? Wise men, tell us.
Do you drink beer in heaven? Learned men, proclaim.
    O happiness! Our shining light.
    O happiness! Our beautiful flower [bright].
You are Mother and Home. Appear, reveal yourself.

The learned men are all silent! The birds also are all mute.
They do not say where mother is, we do not know.
    O happiness and so forth.

There is no happiness in the world. There is no happiness in heaven.
It has not been stashed in a corner.
        You need to look elsewhere.
    O happiness and so forth.

Heaven, earth and moon, all the stars—farewell!
All of you to me are an awful harbor,
        do not expect anything in advance.
    O happiness and so forth.

---

65   Songs of Solomon 1:7.

I have passed all the heavens, so that I might find it in the distance.
And the entire inferno, so that I might meet it.
> O happiness and so forth.

Behold my favorite! A swift young deer jumps.
Higher than the heavens, than the mountains,
> my lily is pure, new and green.
> O happiness! Our bright light!
> O happiness! Our beautiful flower bright!

You are Mother and Home. I see today! Today I hear!

Its voice is sweetness, its eyes light blue.
All is love and the city of Sharon,[66] crystal arms.
> O happiness and so forth.

Do not touch me, for you will meet me,
Do not seek me from without, for you will find me.
> O happiness and so forth.

Ah! Return your gaze to me. It will give wings to me.
Higher than the elements, higher than mountains.
> It will adorn me with feathers.
> O happiness and so forth.

Let us sit down, my brother, sit down to talk.
Your living word is sweet, it purifies all woes for me.
> O happiness! Our bright light!
> O happiness! Our beautiful flower bright!color?

You are Mother and Home. I see you today and hear you.

---

66 A city in the upper basin of the Euphrates, known for its lush vegetation. See Matthew 6: 28 and Luke 12:27. Also note from Songs of Solomon 2:1: "I am the rose of Sharon, and the lily of the valleys".

At noon you sleep in the mountains,
> you tend your flock near the lilies,

Not in the fields of the Gergesenes[67] or its vales.
> O happiness and so forth.

The End.

---

[67] See Matthew 8: 28. A rich land where Christ performed the miracle of making a demon-possessed man well.

TWENTY-SECOND SONG

"Remember your end, and you will not sin."[68] *"There is a way which seemeth right unto a man; but the end thereof are the ways of death."*[69]

Set your gaze out to the distance and the wise rays of light.
And always remember the ultimate end.
Will the arrow strike at
              the certain target of all your matters?
Observing the limit of all your desires,
On what foundation have you built your home?
If on stone, the house will remain whole.
If on sand, stand in a chorus with you and yours,
For a whirlwind will sweep it from the face of the earth.

All flesh is sand and all glory worldly,
All its sweetness becomes loathsome.
Love the narrow path. Avoid the common custom.
May your Lord be joined with David,
If you need to return to Zion,
Then why must you descend to the world?
The path to Jericho is dangerous.
Live in the city that is mother to us all.

---

68   Sirach 7:36 (KJV). I have opted for an exact translation of Skovoroda's inexact quotation. In the OCS and Russian Synodal Bible, this is Sirach 7:39: "поминай последняя твоя, и во веки не согрешиши." In the KJV this is translated as "remember the end, and thou shalt never do amiss."

69   Proverbs 14:12.

If you have taken this road,
May God more quickly obstruct the path!
For you know that having descended into a great abyss,
Our mind will give no joy to us in the abyss of evils.
O you! Who are of the same spirit
And whose number of years does not diminish,
You, knead in us the spirit of the good thief!
Let your storm destroy the net.

                                                                 The End.

TWENTY-THIRD SONG

From this:
"...their days did he consume in vanity...."[70]
"Redeeming the time..."[71] "Celebrate and understand...."[72]

O dearest time of life!
How we do not relish you!
Thus, like an extra burden,
We rush everywhere without looking!
As though past time will return to us.
As though rivers will return to their sources.
As though there were extra years in our hands.
As though our lifetime were comprised of endless days.

For what reason do we wish to live
Eight hundred years on the earth
If we waste them
On all manner of useless things?
Better to live honestly a single hour than wickedly a whole day.
Better to have a single holy day out of a Godless year.
Better to have one year of purity than ten wicked ones.
Better to be of use for ten years
        than an entire lifetime without fruit.

---

[70]   Psalms 77 (78):33.

[71]   Ephesians 5:16.

[72]   Psalms 44 (45):11. Skovoroda is quoting from Psalm 45:11 of the OCS Bible, so I have directly translated from that version instead of quoting from the KJV. Neither the Russian Synodal nor the KJV contain the same opening of the psalm as the OCS version.

Dear friend, abandon sloth,
Cut short even a small amount of harm.
At this moment take up your task:
There! There! Time will float away.
It is not our time that passed us by.
It is not our time that the future will bear.
Only the day today is ours, but not tomorrow's hour.
We do not know what the sunset Glow will bring.

If you do not know how to live,
Then study this figure.
O! Not everyone can accommodate
The common sense of that cleverness.
I know our life is filled with trifling nonsense.
I know the dumbest creature in the world is man.
I know the more he lives, the worse of a fool he becomes.
I know that he who piles up time[73] for himself is blind.

                                                              The End.

---

73   One philosopher was asked what he considered most precious? He answered: time [Skovoroda's note in Latin]. The original reads: Rogatus quidam Philosophus: quid esset praetiosissimum? Resp[ondet]: Tempus.

TWENTY-FOURTH SONG

Of the Roman prophet Horace, translated into the Little Russian dialect in 1765. It begins thusly: "Otium divos rogat in patenti..." and so forth.—It contains a good approach to a peaceful life.

O heavenly peace of ours!
        Where have you hidden yourself from our eyes?
You are beloved by everyone as a rule,
        you have divided us to take different paths.

Behind you sails billow in sailing ships,
So that these wings might find you in foreign lands.

They march behind you, tearing cities asunder,
They bomb for a whole century, but will they ever reach you?

It seems sorrow lives more in larger homes,
A small home is more peaceful
        if it is filled just with essential things.

Ah, we are never satisfied with anything!
        This is the source of all sorrows!
A mind filled with various undertakings,
        that is the source of rebellions!

Let us hold back the insatiable spirit!
        Enough of tormenting a brief lifetime.
What will a land of glory give us?
        You will also be a person.

Sadness flies everywhere to weave its way,
>   along the earth, along the water,
Faster than any lightning,
>   this [frightening] demon can find us anywhere.

We will be happy with the way
>   God made us, driving away sorrow with jest,
Be done with worms eating us,
>   after all there is a chalice for everyone.

Glorious, for example, are heroes, but they lie killed in the fields.
If someone lives long in peace, he suffers in his old age.

God blessed you with good land, but in an instant it can be gone.
My lot is cast with beggars, for God gave us part of his wisdom.

>   The End.
>   *"Nihil est ab omni Parte beatum."*
>   *There is a chalice for all people.*

TWENTY-FIFTH FAREWELL SONG

On the departure of Father Hervasy Yakubovych, who is moving from Pereyaslav to Bilhorod to the archimandrite's and judicial rank in 1758. From this seed: "The Lord shall preserve thy going out and thy coming in from this time forth, and even for evermore."[74]

    You are on a journey, do you want to leave us?
    Ride happy, whole and healthy [without a fuss]!
    May the winds be favorable for you,
    Slight, warm and not too cold, [too].
May your path from here be happy.

    Your fears of the road will disappear.
    Sleep, roadside dust, [show no fear].
    Let your swift compliant horses
    Carry you as though along your palm,
Along a happy trail as though along smooth ice.

    Clouds be gone, you are unsettling!
    Do not pour down, boundless rain!
    Do not light a mid-day campfire.
    Illuminated by the light of the moon,
Be happy this journey, everywhere this night.

    He who gave us the land and roads
    Will guide your stride.
    Brightly sitting up on high [today],

---

[74] Psalms 120(121):8.

His eye watching over your way.
This entrance will bless this happy departure.

Rejoice, happy land!
You will be receiving a good man.
Cast away your jealous habits!
Faithful is he ,who comes to know him.
Happy for a step, happy for a blessed end.

The End.

TWENTY-SIXTH SONG

To Bishop Ioann Kozlovych, who enters the city of Pereyaslav at the rank of Bishop in 1753. From this seed: "May your light shine before the people who saw your good deeds...."[75]

Hasten, Guest! Hurry up!
Crown our wishes.
Like splendid music that you hear,
The spirit moves the body with sweetness [near],
Hence your arrival expected by all
Has uplifted the whole city and people.

Sorrowful city! O, Pereyaslav!
Often recognizing your orphanhood,
Be wary of betraying the most high.
Illumine this bright day for you!
Your ship has been frantic along the waves.
Behold your navigator once again in the ship.

He will make right your path to the heavens,
Presenting the light of Christ's words.
In Him you will see the fruit of the spirit,
Like in the mirror of transparent waters,
For the lamb following Christ?
Humbly will cleanse impurity.

Both with deed and language
He will make your spirit whole that is poisoned by sin.

---

75   According to a note in the Ushkalov edition of Skovoroda (#148, p. 110), this is an inexact quotation from Psalms 79(80): 15-16.

To what amount of honest flesh is the spirit,
To what amount of the earthly is the heavenly circle,
To what amount the enemy of the soul's passions
Be better than the healers of the flesh.

Christ! Holy spring of blessings.
Pour out your sprit onto the shepherd.
Be an example for him.
So that in looking at him every man
Would enter his flock,
And extend him a happy life.

                                                                 The End.

CARMEN

In Imaginem Beatissimae Virginis, concipientis Christum, calcantis Sphaeram Mundi, decrescentem Lunam, et Serpentem, cum suo Pomo146 . Haec Imago stat in Ludo Theologico in Urbe Zacharpoli. Formatum hoc carmen Anno 1760, cum essem Ludi Poetici Magister.

Picta stat ecce vides Virgo castissima! cujus
    Pomum, Anguis, Mundus, Lunaque sub Pedibus
Nempe Voluptates Carnis, Pomum illud adumbrat,
    Ad quas, ceu Serpens, allicit ipsa Caro.
Errorum Vulgi male sani, Mundus Imago est.
    At Bona fluxa, suo Nomine Luna notat.
Quatuor haec vince! et capies in corpore Christum.
    Vivere in impuro Corde, Sophia nequit.

MELODY

To the icon of the Immaculate Conception, with the sphere of the world beneath her feet, a waning moon, and a serpent with its apple. This icon is hanging in the School of Theology in Kharkiv. This Melody was created in 1760 when I was a teacher in the school of poetry.

Behold! This is the Virgin standing, pure in womb!
    An apple, serpent, the world,
        and the moon beneath her feet.
Base pleasures of the flesh are her apple,
    To which this flesh, sly and
        charming as a serpent, drags you.
The circle of the world forms a wicked assortment of notions,
    As the moon is the shadow
        and sign of worldly possessions.
Be victorious! And Christ will abide in you.
    Be like the Virgin, pure:
        wisdom will not accommodate earthly pleasures.

M.G.s.s.s.

TWENTY-SEVENTH SONG

To the Bilhorod Bishop Ioasaf Mytkevych, who visited the garden of the seminary school in Kharkiv. From this seed: "Return, we beseech thee, O God of hosts: look down from heaven, and behold, and visit this vine...."[76] "But the fruit of the Spirit is love, joy, peace, and so forth."[77]

Holy garden of heavenly learning!
Pink leaves and your beautiful blossoms.
Take upon yourself the look of spring.
A bright light has illuminated you.
The spirit, breathing, blesses you from high.
Rejoice, o regiment of trees!
The entire throng of all, great and small.

Shepherd of ours! Image[78] of Christ!
Of those blessed, meek, kind, [and right].
Spotless mirror of goodness!
Carry your fine legs, prepared
To bless our steadfast world.
Gaze upon this blessed stronghold.
Low he waits for help from you.
He gives you his heart and hands.

Water the garden, this holy garden,
With the current of pious waters
From the very springs of the apostles.

---

76   Psalms 79(80):15.

77   Galatians 5:22.

78   Image can also be read as "icon" here.

  Do not allow the poison of heresies.
  Cast away all manner of false kings,
  And may it give birth to kings of the spirit,
Kingdom of the king, encompassing everyone,
Hell's scepter, overcoming sin.

  May your bright gaze look upon it!
  In your never sleeping gaze,
  Not even a leaf will fall from it.
  Not a leaf on it will be bare,
  Hypocritically flattering, but soon
  It will bring all the fruit of the spirit.
Faith, peace, joy, meekness, love,
And all manner of holy things.

  Thus from you yourself king of kings,
  And holy people ask just this.
  And what is dearer to you than this?
  What is the best gift that Christ brings?
  This is the first gift, the holiest of holies,
  That the shepherd brings to his flock.
He will strengthen you for deed
And will uphold your holy life indeed.

               The End.

Pro Memoria, i.e., a note for the sake of memory. This hierarch was born near Kyiv in the village of Kozelets. He was an enlightened pastor, meek, kind, forgiving, truth-loving, an altar of feeling, a lantern of love. In the garden of this true gardener of Christ I hallowedly and piously spent three years: 1760 and 1763-1764, during which he passed away from the earth to the heavens with my secret love. He was a doer. I was amazed by his insightful, generous and pure heart. For the sake of this in the name of all, who love God and God's books, and friends of God, in memory of and gratitude to him, this good friend of God and mankind, to whom I bring this song of mine as a Peter's pence.

Lover of the Holy Bible Hryhory Var-Sava Skorovoda

TWENTY-EIGHTH SONG

About the mysterious core and eternal joy of God-loving hearts. From these seeds: "The heart's desire is the life of man, and the joy of a man is many-dayed" [79]; "and whosoever shall lose his life shall preserve it."[80] "For what is a man profited, if he shall gain the whole world, and lose his own soul?"[81]

Ascend to the heavens, even to the forests of Versailles.
    Don your golden raiments,
    Even don a king's hat [for sure].
When unhappy, you are naked and poor.

Live as long as 300 years, live even through the entire world.
    What will help you then [abide]
    If your heart sobs inside?
When unhappy, you're just naked and dead.

Conquer the entire earthly sphere, be a king for many nations.
    What will help you abide
    If your heart sobs inside?
When you are unhappy, you are just naked and vile.

I should forget about thinking, if you will!
    How many live on the moon?
    Forget about Copernicus's spheres!

---

79   Psalms 20 (21):1-5. I have been unable to locate an exact Biblical citation for this line, although all the imagery in Skovoroda's quotation seems to come from these five verses of this Psalm.

80   Luke 17:33.

81   Matthew 16:26.

Gaze into the caves of the heart!
In your soul is the word. Lo you will be happy with IT!

God is the best astronomer, He is the best steward.
    Blessed mother nature
    Does not create anything foolishly.
What you need most you'll find inside your self.

Gaze, if you will, inside yourself! You will find a friend within.
    There you will find a second freedom,
    In a wicked fate you'll find a blessed one.
In your prison there is light, in your filth there is a flower.

Augustine sang the truth, there is no hell and never was.
    Your accursed will—that is hell,
    Our will is the hearth of our hell.
Cut away that freedom, friend, then there will be no hell or pain.

Freedom! O insatiable hell!
        All are food for you, and you are poison to all.
    Day and night your jaws gape,
    Without even looking you will devour everything.
Kill that soul, brother! This way you will empty all hell.

Lord! O living Word! Who can be happy without you?
    You alone are life and joy for all,
    You alone are heaven and sweetness for all!
Kill the evil will inside us! Let your VOICE rule!

Give us this most necessary gift. We glorify you, king of kings.
    The entire Universe sings praise to you,
    You are created in this Law.
The necessary is not difficult, the difficult not necessary.

PRO MEMORIA, or a remembrance.

> *The most essential of Augustine's words are these:*
> *"Tolle Voluntatem propriam*
> *Et tolletur Infernus. Or:*
> *Eliminate your own will,*
> *And Hell will be eliminated.*

As it is in seed the Oak of Mamre,[82] so in his sharp word was hidden the entire heights of the Theological pyramid and as the abyss with its muzzle swallowed the entire River Jordan of God's wisdom. Man's will and God's are two gates: of Hell and Heaven. Having discovered amid the sea God's will of his will, find *kifa*, that is, its harbor: "Upon this rock I will build my entire Church."[83] "It is hidden to them like the heavens"[84] and so forth. "And the earth (this is its promise! Look, man) amid the water...."[85] For who transformed his will into the will of God, singing this praise: "My heart is smitten"[86] and so forth, for God himself is the heart. He is free will, the heart, love,

---

82 Abraham lived in the Mamre plain in Hebron (Genesis 13:18) where he built an altar to God. The Oak of Mamre is also called the Oak of Abraham. It is the spot in the Bible where three angels come to Abraham.

83 Matthew 16:18, The precise KJV quote is: "upon this rock I will build my church."

84 From 2 Peter 3:5. The OCS Bible has this as "Таится бо им сие хотящим, яко небеса" and in the KJV: "For this they willingly are ignorant of, that by the word of God the heavens were of old." I've opted for a more exact translation of the original OCS version, from which Skorovoda quotes elliptically.

85 Paraphrase of Genesis 1:6. In the KJV this is: "And God said, Let there be a firmament in the midst of the waters, and let it divide the waters from the waters.'

86 This is from Psalm 102:4 (KJV) and 101:5 from the OCS Bible.

God, spirit, paradise, a harbor, blessedness, eternity too. He does not rebel, having his heart: "His will guides everything."[87] Augustine's word breathes with this: "Rend your heart."[88] "Take my yoke upon you."[89] "Mortify your bodily passions."[90] "...ye cannot do the things that ye would."[91] "For we wrestle not against flesh and blood."[92] "A man's enemies are the men of his own house."[93] "Thou shalt tread upon an asp and basilisk."[94] "It shall bruise thy head"[95] and so forth.

---

87   A paraphrase of Revelations 4:11. In the KJV this is: "Thou art worthy, O Lord, to receive glory and honour and power: for thou hast created all things, and for thy pleasure they are and were created."

88   Joel 2:13. In the KJV this is: "And rend your heart, and not your garments, and turn unto the Lord your God: for he is gracious and merciful, slow to anger, and of great kindness, and repenteth him of the evil."

89   Matthew 11:29. "Take my yoke upon you, and learn of me; for I am meek and lowly in heart: and ye shall find rest unto your souls."

90   Inexact quote from Colossians 3:5. In the KJV this is: "Mortify therefore your members which are upon the earth; fornication, uncleanness, inordinate affection, evil concupiscence, and covetousness, which is idolatry."

91   Galatians 5:17. In KJV this is: "For the flesh lusteth against the Spirit, and the Spirit against the flesh: and these are contrary the one to the other: so that ye cannot do the things that ye would."

92   Ephesians 6:12. In the KJV this is: "For we wrestle not against flesh and blood, but against principalities, against powers, against the rulers of the darkness of this world, against spiritual wickedness in high places."

93   Micah 7:6.

94 Psalms 90(91): 13, The KJV differs slightly, so I have translated directly from Skovoroda's original here. The KJV version is: "Thou shalt tread upon the lion and adder: the young lion and the dragon shalt thou trample under feet."

95   Genesis 3:15.

TWENTY-NINTH SONG

> *To this end: "They controlled the storms"[96] and so forth. "What manner of man is this! for he commandeth even the winds and water, and they obey him."[97]*

The storm's whirlwind sways my boat,
Behold it tosses me first to the abyss! Then upward!
    O, there is no peace for me today!
    O, I have no helmsman.
Behold the sea is swallowing me!

The mountain rises to the heavens,
Another descends to the abyss,
    Hope melts away for me,
    My soul disappears.
I waited—there is no help!

O comfortable harbor!
Quietly, sweetly, without slander!
    O Son of Mary!
    You alone be
The shore to my ship.

You lie asleep in my ship.
Arise! Listen to my lament!
    O! Hold back the sea.

---

[96] Psalms 106 (107):29. In the KJV this is: "He maketh the storm a calm, so that the waves thereof are still."

[97] Luke 8:25.

    Give me help soon.
O! Arise, my glory!

Deliver me from disaster,
Calm earthly passions in my soul.
    They torment my spirit!
    And afflict my life.
Save me, Peter, I pray!

The End.

Composed in 1785, the 17th day
of September, in the village
of Velyky Burluk.

THIRTIETH SONG

From this ancient verse:[98]
Thz vraz apolane. Taku gar panta gpraokei.
En Jeroz ez erifon tracun enhce tragov.
That is:
Enjoy your days, for all that is young grows old:
In just one summer a kid becomes a shaggy goat.

Fall passes us, and spring has passed,
A mother goat gives birth to a kid at the arrival of spring.
The summer has barely heated up and the kid has become a goat,
    A bearded billygoat.
Ah, let us renounce sorrows!
        Ah, our lifetime, so short and minute!
    Life be sweet!

Whoever forever carries sadness in the womb
Has never lived and lies in a tomb.
Ah, comfort and joy! O sweetness of the heart!
    Life you are true [from the start].
Not beautiful in span, but beautiful in goodness [of a man],
Such is life, like a song.

Merciful God is alive, and I love Him.
For me he is a firm rock, sweetly I endure sorrow.
He is alive, undying, my living soul lives
    With Him.

---

[98]   Note #78 in Hryhoryi Skovoroda, *Tvory u dvokh tomakh*, I (Kyiv, 1994): 469, observes that Skovoroda found this Greek epigram in the library of the Holy Trinity-St. Sergius Monastery near Moscow.

For whomever He does not serve, let that poor orphan
> Rightly mourn.

Do you want to live in sweetness? Do not be envious anywhere.
> Be sated with a small portion, do not fear everywhere.
Put out of your mind the dust of the grave and childhood fears;
> Death is peace, not harm [that is near].
Thus lived the Athenian, thus lived the Hebrew
> Epicure—Christ.

The End.

Composed during the opening of the Kharkiv vicarate when I was wandering about at the Sennyansky Monastery.

Hryhory Varsava Skovoroda.

Other Poems and Songs

DE LIBERTATE

What is freedom? What good is there in it?
    Some say it is golden.
Ah, but it's not golden, if you compare gold
    To freedom, it's just mud all told.
O, if only I'd not become befooled,
    Unable to be without my freedom [of old].
Glory to you forever, o chosen man,
    Father of freedom, hero-Bohdan![99]

---

[99] Bohdan Khmelnytsky (1595-1657), elected Hetman (chief leader) of the Ukrainian Kozaks in 1648. He led the Kozaks in wars primarily against Poland and Russia, eventually concluding a peace treaty with Russia at Pereyaslav in 1654. Khmelnytsky was considered a hero-figure in Skovoroda's time. In later times, the great poet Taras Shevchenko in particular and many other Ukrainians later saw Khmelnytsky as someone, who led Ukraine to ruin by signing the treaty with Russia.

FABULA

Just as the sun had fallen toward evening
Everywhere the Heavens had turned dark,
On the firmament beautiful stars glimmered
Like Precious Diamonds,
Thales[100] cries out: "My kind old woman!"
"Why are you screaming, foolish Sage?"
"I'm tired of sitting on this spot.
Take me somewhere to gaze at the stars."
The kind old woman started off before him,
And behind her the foolish Sage followed.
They walked toward a high-high Hill from where
They could see the circle of stars.
"O," the Sage shouted out, "I'm doomed, old woman!"
The poor man had fallen into a hole, tearing off his ear.
"You wouldn't have fallen into a ditch, slow-witted grandpa,
Why didn't you follow my tracks?
Not seeing the ditch right in front of your nose,
How can you know the stars, dim-witted one?"
From these speculations the old woman
Led the Sage back home without his ear.

---

[100] Thales of Miletus (ca. 624BC-ca. 546BC), one of the Seven Sages of Ancient Greece.

FABULA DE TANTALO[101]

King Tantalus once invited the master of the Gods Jove
To a king's Feast at his home.
Jove, knowing the ways of Politics,
Invited Tantalus for Heavenly victuals in return.
But the Heavenly Victuals spoiled Tantalus!
And Jove did not want to just let
His Dear Guest go without a gift.
He said: "Ask for whatever you want on your way out!"
"Let me dine here eternally,"
Tantalus answered. Jove was insulted
That Tantalus was not ashamed of asking for this,
But, remembering his noble word,
Said the road was prepared for him.
From that time on Tantalus began to feast in heaven.
And what isn't there at the heavenly table?
Here there are various wines, sweet Nectar
That sweetens godly palates,
Here there is Ambrosia, the victuals of the higher gods,
Next to it, regal suppers seem like nothing.
Everywhere roses turn crimson before your eyes,
Incense is burned everywhere here.
Sweet-voiced Muses shout throughout the Hall,
Handsome Ganymede serves everything himself;
The lover of Bacchus dances comically.
All kinds of jesters jest delightfully.

---

101 Mythological hero and favorite of the gods, whom Jupiter eventually sent to Hades for his excessive pride.

And though dall-Oglio[102] never sang in this Choir,
A hundred Apollos are better than this one.
In short: all corporeal feelings
There delighted in wondrous sweets.
Sitting, Tantalus continues to gaze agreeably,
He sighs, though all is abundant,
He wrinkles his face, fear grates his limbs,
He's startled as though the devil had taken him.
What's the reason? Throughout the mansion above
An enormous stone hangs low
Above his very head,
And does not allow him to sit in peace.
He's afraid, poor man, that if he moves it,
It's hanging on a hair, and right there will crush him into dust.

---

102   Domenico dall-Oglio, Italian composer, who in 1735 served in the court of Empress Elizabeth of Russia during Skovoroda's time spent in the court capella choir.

FABULA

A certain old man named Filaret lived his whole life [alone]
In a wasteland in the depths of an oak grove.
A fine young man named Filidon,
Made his way to the bearded old man,
Having heard from many about him,
That the hermit monk was holy and brimming with wisdom.
When he greeted the earnest gray-bearded man,
"Be well!" The old man said: "And you, son."
"Do not be angry, merciful father,
Tell me which life path is holy and resolute?
My mother and father have forsaken me,
Long ago I held their wake.
Please be my parent in their place,
And you will be, if you will be my teacher."
"Son, I myself have scant wisdom,
I only know the path of life is hard."
"Be so kind, o gray-headed man,
I will remember everything, I am not a fur filled with holes."
"It's dangerous, son, to travel around the world,
As long as you are alive, you need to struggle with the world.
Learn from the experience of others,
And not from your woes know the bad from the good.
For instance, if you see that a thief is beaten,
Learn from him that stealing – soon leads to woe.
Do not befriend someone incapable of goodness,
For you can only be saintly with one who is saintly.
More so, do not do what weathervanes do,
But what the laws of reason command you.
He, who is partial to this world's mores,
Can not be poor in the world."

Filidon, upon seeing the old man saying things
Counter to his thoughts suddenly felt bored.
I am grateful, old gray-haired man."
"Go with God, my son." He left on his way.
Sacred is this wisdom, though not affected,
He thinks to himself. Later, searching for a friend
Of his own feather, marched in scholarly
Directions, so as to make his mind perfected.
They took the young swain by force to Prussia,
Where there was a war against the French.
And when a dozen years had passed,
Fate impelled this Ulysses home.
He marched right into the forest to Filaret,
Recalling the old man's wise decrees.
"Save me, father!" "Who are you?"
"Do you remember, holy father, Filidon?"
"Ah, my have you become a person with affectations!"
"The storm of the world has wearied me."
"What kind of cover is that on your right eye?"
"A bullet knocked it out with a contusion."
"What is that awful hole on your brow?"
"Smashed by a rifle." "And what are those two scars
On your cheek?" "I got that wound in a fight."
"At the front?" "Oh no! In a tavern while drinking."
"A piece of your nose seems to be dangling."
 "It's dangling: because it was sliced by a Frenchman."
"And you have splotches all over your face." "Those are scabs."
"It, I think, French syphilis, isn't so simple.
You now, son, are walking with a limp."
"I fell from a horse, and twisted my knee.
And besides that the doctors treated me
When that illness clogged up my veins."

"Why have you begun to cry? Crying won't help
Now at all." "O my God, my God!
Oh help me, holy father!"
"I can not now, my dear son!
You heeded not my advice back then,
Now go beg for help from the world."

A conversation about WISDOM

WISDOM AND MAN

Man. Dear sister, or what should I call you?
You are the mother
> of all goodness and harmony,

Tell me your name, tell it to me yourself;
Without you we will have all kinds of foolish thoughts.

Wisdom. Among the Greeks I was called Sophia in ancient times,
And in Russia they call me Wisdom,
But the Romans called me Minerva,
And the good Christian gave me the name Christ.

Man. Tell me, do you dwell in the Chinese lands?

Wisdom. My name is in different words there.

Man. Do you dwell, too, in barbarian lands?

Wisdom. What kind of idiocy, my friend, are you weaving for me?
Without me, my friend, not a single line would be!
And how would I, tell me, not live among the Chinese.
Where night and day abide,
> where there is summer and spring,

I rule everywhere with my father alone.

Man. Tell me, who is your father? Don't be angry with a fool.

Wisdom. Come to know me first,
> then you will come to know my father.

Man. Tell me, reveal how you dwell with the Chinese?

Wisdom. Exactly the way as I do here: I look, who is mine, is mine.

Man. Only the dead must live there.

Wisdom. My sister is lying to you, it's the same as here.

Man. Do you really have a sister?

Wisdom. Yes, I do
Have a sister, the way day has the night.

Man. And does she always lie?
 Even though she's your only sister?
Wisdom. Though we have a single father,
 the children aren't the same.
Man. What is her name?
Wisdom. She has a hundred names. She,
 However, among the Russians is *beztolkovshchina*.[103]
Man. Does she have horns?
Wisdom. Fool!
Man. Or with a beard?
 Or is she in a cowl?
Wisdom. You're lying! If you wish,
 She will enter into your make-up. Ah you!
 Disappear from here!
 Next to you I am like night next to the light.
Man. Better that you disappear! Out of the sight of my eyes!
 You yourself are a fool, if you've given in to deception.
 You're lying about everything that you can't hear anywhere.
 And, truthfully to say, you're singing absurdity.
 The people here have been born and educated not this way,
 To willingly listen to your wild lies.
 Maybe one or two can be found
 Who will like your wild idea.

---

103 Confusion, disorder.

* * *

You still wrinkle your face, you're always sad,
Can you call this life?
He lives better who always looks cheerful,
Who brightly leads his life without gloom.
He who is sad, incessantly yearns,
Drawn-out death stifles this one.

In Praise of Astronomy Ex Ovid[ii] Fast[orum] l[ibris]

Happy are those who still in old age have endeavored
    To maintain reason and to watch
        the cycle of movement of the stars.
You can believe that they have left all earthly trifles behind,
    That they have risen in heart to the heavenly mountains.
The comforts of the flesh have not distracted their hearts,
    Neither the labors of warriors, nor stately concerns,
Neither flighty glory, nor empty honors,
    Alluring flatteries are baser than boundless riches.
Before our eyes they arose, they've become famous
    And subjected the flow of the stars to their mind.
This way one should rise to the mountainous circles.
    Not the way the ancient Titans walked in fear of the gods.

O delicati blanda etc.[104]

O dear rustic, beloved peace of mine!
    Bereft of all sorrows.
O the sound of springs gurgling water!
    O dark, chilly forest!
O rustling curls of sylvan locks!
    O the beautiful green on meadows!
O Mother-solitude for heavenly thoughts!
    O sad, awful quietude,
Where only a bird's voice truly gives freedom,
    And a shepherd's flute,
As he herds the sheep into the fragrant field,
    Or herds them back home again!
O my dear little table, covered with simple
    Rustic dishes and not extravagant ones!
Not those that will when luxurious taste,
    Flavored by a hired chef,
For the sons with their father return from plowing,
    Their mother cooks alone in the house.
O library, you are my chosen one!
    O the books are known to so few!
O tiny room that fits only one!
    O dream free and pleasant!
O the path to bliss is sure and well-known!
    O the path for those of the world is unknown!
When I seek you alone, when my spirit burns,
    For I scorn all else at once.
When all kinds of people run to you, they honor you.
    Over all the riches of the world,

---

104   O tender, dear, etc. The poem is an imitation of French poet Marc Antoine Murier's (1526-1588) Latin verse. [*Tvory* I (1994), p. 473].

Who with water of the spirit washed away dirt from the eyes
    And tasted true wisdom.
You, my friend, are capable of drinking the heavenly water,
    To which this unclean world is alien,
Whether you pull in one tug, or are tormented by the evil moth
    Of glory and richness,
Do you honor the servitude of courtly life
    More than rural pleasures and sweet peace?
O, I ask you for the sake of the mountains of Zion,
    Which mountain you have seen
        from your earliest childhood,
Kindly take advice from an old man,
    Which he himself took, but not in time.
Who beckons you from books and from freedom,
    Know that those souls are flatterers,
Know that the poison of deceit
        is hidden beneath the honey of words.
    Avoid those souls, having covered over your ears.
The blessed one lives not in golden metal,
    Nor in Indian Pearls,
A heart that is not greedy will be sated by little,
    Nothing will sate greed.
How can you live life in the world
    Quietly, sweetly and freely,
Then tell me, which demon began to chase you from there
    To accept the chains willingly?
And in life to look at someone else's freedom,
    Fluttering to the gazes of the wealthy?
Well, untie the knots, knock off the yoke,
    Be your quick giver of freedom!
Dare to be happy, be free from everything,
    That which nails the mind to the earth,
And steaming upward, where the home is full of space,

   And all he thinks about are eternal things,
Surprisingly leaving the gifts of blind happiness
   For all the fools in this world to wonder.
And if only in my blossoming years of youth
   And not in this age of gray,
An old friend, who was astute, could relate with sense
   What your friend was now explaining,
Then I now wouldn't so bemoan in vain
   The many years I lost in the service of the court!

IN NATALEM IESU[105]

O new, wondrous, miraculous Night,
Brighter than the light at noon,
When, through the dark black gloom
The perpetual light of the sun shone.
> Rejoice, for God is with us,
> For God is with us.[106]

The one who calms all the seas,
Who measures all of us for God,
Today in a squalid cattle shed
Teaches us all the lesson of poverty.
> Rejoice, for God is with us. (2 times)

There near the Town of Bethlehem,
Shepherds herding their flock
Are the first to hear good tidings
From the Angels, that Christ is coming
> To the earth, for God is with us. (2)

You can see how beloved to God
Is that gentle, unpolished simplicity,
That earnestly keeps righteousness
Through its simple, ancient, faithful ways.
> Rejoice! For God is with you. (2)

---

105 In English: For the birth of Jesus.
106 From Isaiah 8: 10.

There next to the Town of Bethlehem
A throng of shepherds tended their flocks [...]¹⁰⁷

To the tone: "Let us praise Christ the King!"

---

107 According to note #5 in the Ushkalov Skovoroda edition (p. 136), the poem breaks off in Skovoroda's manuscript here.

EST QUAEDAM MAERENTI FLERE VOLUPTAS[108]

Who will give me tears, who will give the rain today?
Who will give the sea? Who will give the tearful rivers?
    I weep over sin
    Without rest
    And wash it
    In many-watered
        Unstoppable tears.
The hellish flame of my sins dried out my eyes;
And like a diamond my heart is hardened.
    To carry the teary stream for me,
    So that I can vomit out
    The illnesses
    Grown cold inside me
        From there.
You, who opens wide the passages
        for the streams in the mountains,
From on high in heaven you lower high waters;
    Fill up eyes,
    Pour out enough,
    Touch the heart,
    Allow us to feel,
        Father of consolations!
And I will be affluent with these teary streams,
For me they will be my only kind consolations.
    Even your stupidity
    Is Wisdom over the World,
    And wail over laughter,
    His consolations,
        Wondrous God!

---

108   In English: In grief tears bring a certain consolation.

QUID EST VIRTUS?[109]

It is difficult to conquer anger and other passions,
    It is difficult not to give into the lusty passions of the flesh,
It is difficult to bear reproach from everyone for nothing,
    It is difficult to leave your beloved homeland for Christ.
It is difficult to take reason from
        the earth to the heavenly Mountains,
    It is difficult not to drown in this abyss of the World.
Whosoever can conquer this ancient devilry
    Is a king, a sovereign, mighty in spiritual strength.

---

109   In English: What is virtue?

AN EPIGRAM

Tell me briefly the deed of a wise Man!
Keep Light in your mind and Health in your body.

SIMILITUDINES EX VIRG[ILIO]
2. AENEIDE

Similitudo clamantis Laoco[o]ntis, circumplicati a draconibus.

> What terrifying roars he releases,
>> When the near dead wild bull
>>> runs away from the high priest.

Simil[itudo] Aeneae spectantis ex super domo sua incendium Trojae.

> Thus, like fire in the plowed field he
>> will fall during cruel storms
>> Or the swift rainy flow from tall mountains
> Breaks fields and beautiful sowing, spreading,
>> And rushing it drags forests,
>>> falling into a stupor without knowing,
> The shepherd upon hearing the rustling above the cliffs.

Simil[tudo] Aeneae, quomodo Trojae noctu cum sociis
>> in medium hostium sese conjecit.

> ...Afterward in that minute
> Like predatory wolves, which fierce hunger
>> has blindly chased out
> Of pits into the dark night,
>> at home the tribe waits
> Alone, gaping voraciously;
>> through fire, right through a sword
> We run toward imminent death.

Quomodo Androgeus imprudenter noctu in hostes resiliit.

> He grew petrified and tore suddenly back with words.
> So that someone amid
> the prickly plant unexpectedly
> Stepped on a snake and suddenly
> turned pale, running away,
> But it grows angry, raising its neck with poison.

Quale certamen int[er] Aeneam et nobiliss[imum]
Graecorum super Helena.

> Since when the winds began to rush in foul weather
> In a stormy whirlwind from the west,
> south and east,
> Forests then crackle, agitated waves seethe
> With sand and fly to bottomless places.

Cui similis erat Pyrrhus, cum in[ter] ceteros oppugnaret regiam Priami.

> What serpent, when it came out
> into the world full of poison,
> That hid beneath the earth in the time of wintry cold,
> Taking off its skin on a day of beautiful spring,
> It curls its spine into a circle,
> along which there is a clear shine,
> And raising its slippery chest up,
> tossing a frenzied steel sword gaze,
> It hisses with its three-pronged
> tongue from its mouth.

IN NATALEM BASILII TOMARAE, PUERI 12 ANNORUM[110]

The yearly circle is complete and again has begun. Today
>We have the first day, the beginning of the new year,

You were destined, gifted boy Vasyl,
>To be born on this day. This is good news for you.

From your parents you were born into
>>the world, lad, the first sprout.

>The first with virtue throughout, be the first in glory,

The first of strong mind, and the first with this natural gift
>That your corporeal beauty requires.

Nature has sent blessings to you, first-born,
>That for younger children was a stern step-mother.

This way the universal source, creating Adam first,
>Then created Eve, the smaller in his love.

I joyously congratulate you,
>>that so much good has been given to you:

>Merciful God has bestowed so much upon you.

Just heigh-ho! How richly the Creator has consigned to you,
>In time He will want to take much in return from you.

Thus, take up and do not shun all manner of learning and work,
>And not just in name, but in actions Vasyl.

---

[110] On the birthday of Vasily Tomara, a twelve-year-old boy. According to a note in the Ushkalov Skovoroda edition (p. 145), Tomara (1746/7-1814) became an important diplomat for the Russian Empire.

ON THE BIRTHDAY OF THE BISHOP OF BILHOROD[111]

Although there are countless unpleasant perils in this life,
    We wish you many happy years nonetheless.
Pastor, happily live as long as possible for us and for you.
    Not even if you don't want to live for yourself,
        do live long for others.
Live long happily, so that people will just be joyous for you,
    Father-spiritual leader,
        your life is a treasure for us.

---

[111] Ioasaf Mytkevych.

ON THE HOLY SUPPER, OR ON ETERNITY[112]

With your eyes you see here the wine and bread,
> but with your mind you see God himself,
> Who is hidden as flesh.

He only who is hidden is everlasting,
> the visible is just a dream and a specter:
> To be hidden is something, to be visible—nothing.

Although you can see the machine of the world,
> nonetheless it is just a dream and specter.
> The truly existing things are always hidden beneath it.

When the oak tree casts its tall shadow at sunset,
> Although spread out, all the same it is not an oak tree,

Why do we follow the flesh in turn, which,
> when at times visible, negates existence?
> Why do we flee death? It permits us to be hidden.

When it has hidden us, only then will it allow us to be:
> Reality is always hidden, one can only see its shadow.

Quickly arise, my righteous reason!
> Be resurrected from the shadows!
> Strong, you will overcome all,
> filled with light, you will recover your sight.

Lead me, my light! and this traveling companion will follow.
> This spirit that consecrates its will to you.

You are a ray of the sun unshielded by shadow in your concealment:
> Things do not exist without you
> and neither does the shadow.

You are the body and matter of shadows,
> but to things you are a shadow.
> Thanks to you everything has its own existence.

---

112   I am grateful to Adrian Wanner for his suggestions in comparing my English translations to the original Latin text of this poem.

Therefore, you are always hidden in
>> the shadows distinctly visible to us;
> But in those, which are hidden,
>> we always see you distinctly.

And when you emerge distinctly, the thing or essence that till now
> Had its own existence, loses it at once.

When you vanish, it's not quite completely: for when
>> a thing ceases to be, then its existence begins;
> That is, you are visible again in a new form.

Why do you play with my reason, supple, holy serpent?
> Fleeing, you remain, but remaining you flee.

You are hidden in the shadows, but for things you remain a shadow,
> And when you disappear completely, nothing can be.

Thus, even when you are surrounded with a hundred mirrors,
> In the various mirrors there is really just one form of you.

I am not the one who can capture you, though
>> I try; when I give you back,
> I preserve you, You are whole even when divided in pieces.

Everyone consumes you, but you remain whole.
> Everyone always takes you, though for all you are unknown.

You cannot be anyone's, for you are the one and only for all.
> The more you sate me, the more my hunger grows.

You are the food, concealed today in me, to be a good communicant:
> Your shadow is always ample for small children.

O shrewd serpent! you are hidden like a hook in bait,
> With which you catch many unthinking
>> children for your kingdom!

I praise your cleverness and ardently esteem your trickery,
> Your holiness even sanctifies your shadow.

The caught fish no longer needs tasty bait,
> Thus when I was caught, your shadow was unneeded.

Take off your mask! I've recognized you moving without shadow,
> I could see you up close, for before you were the *lotus* for me.

Strengthened by this, I was able to slaythe erring dogmas
> Of stupidity, which give birth to all kinds of sins.

Filled with this, I could and can subdue fierce passions,
> If you do not deprive me of your trustworthy protection.

Give me peace while I live in the world,
> Be sweet honey for me, my light; my life!

When old age starts to cover my head with gray,
> Yield your last gifts to my tears:

Make me doubly old, both in soul and in body;
> This will happen when you fill my mind with light.

When strength abandons my body, do not abandon my heart
> And mind, my light! My life!

When the comforts of the flesh leave me,
> you be my sumptuous pleasure!
> This will happen when you fill my entire mind with light.

When I no longer have the riches of the flesh,
> you will be a Persian treasure!
> This will happen when you fill my mind with light.

When the rabble begins to curse me, extend benevolence to me!
> This will unfold when you fill my mind with light.

Arise quickly! Why do you not lead me
> from the shadows of things?
> But till then fill my heart with light.

I am ashes, shadow, nothing.
> When you fill me with light, then I will be
> Existing, a thing—not shadow, ashes, nothing.

Lead me away from love of the inert earth:
> Thus there will be peace when your light leads me.

Give me this light, enough for me to scorn death,
> Give me to desire death! Give me to love death!

ON ILLUSORY COMFORT

When the faint shadow disappears,
>the heat will burn you right away;

When a roof covers you, you'll have peace forever.
The passion of the body recently sweetened you with honey,
>As soon as it disappears, the heart fills with bitterness.

Beloved of the gods, flee! The hook is hidden to allure;
>Need when it swiftly flees, leaves the hook just nibbled.

Virtue is not this way, for it makes the soul firm.
>At first like a venom, bitter, after a time sweet, like honey.

This is how you take all the bitter medicines with heavy misfortune,
>Then any kind of food will taste good in time.

Whoever has not given in to a fever that causes dreams, till then
>The confusion of the body quickly turns him back.

Whoever survives a harsh winter will also see that beauty-spring;
>Whoever has sat in the cold should undergo the winter.

God is just everywhere, constantly varying things.
>There are no totally pure things:
>>God created everything green.

For the surface of the bitter is covered with the sweet.
>The beginning
>Of what appears sweet has a bitter end.

And to the contrary, the sweetening
>is covered with dispirited labor,
>And he who consumed the bitter will obtain sweetness.

Only base hearts begin from sweetness:
>Few crown their work with sweetness in the end.

•

CONTENTS

{ page 7 } • A note from the editor and translator

{ page 13 } • A Note on Transliteration

{ page 15 } • Introduction

{ page 39 } • The Garden of Divine Songs

{ page 103 } • Other Poems and Songs

The Complete Correspondence of
HRYHORY SKOVORODA

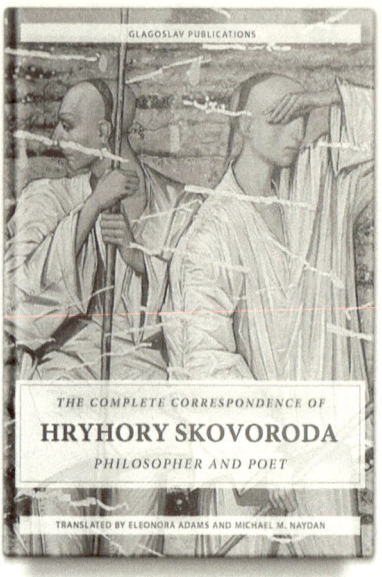

The religious philosopher and poet Hryhory Skovoroda (1722-1794) is described by many as the Ukrainian Socrates and was one of the most learned men of his time. He was a polyglot who knew the Bible virtually by heart, as well as the writings of the Church Fathers and the literature of Greek and Roman antiquity. The eminent literary critic Ivan Dziuba considers Skovoroda the greatest Ukrainian mind ever. And Yuri Andrukhovych, one of the most prominent Ukrainian writers of today, calls him "the first Ukrainian hippie" on account of his itinerant lifestyle and rejection of worldly life. The impact of Skovoroda's life and works has been well documented on major writers in future generations, such as Leo Tolstoy, Andrei Bely and Pavlo Tychyna, to name but a few.

Buy it > www.glagoslav.com

Dear Reader,

Thank you for purchasing this book.

We at Glagoslav Publications are glad to welcome you, and hope that you find our books to be a source of knowledge and inspiration.

We want to show the beauty and depth of the Slavic region to everyone looking to expand their horizon and learn something new about different cultures, different people, and we believe that with this book we have managed to do just that.

Now that you've got to know us, we want to get to know you. We value communication with our readers and want to hear from you! We offer several options:

– Join our Book Club on Goodreads, Library Thing and Shelfari, and receive special offers and information about our giveaways;

– Share your opinion about our books on Amazon, Barnes & Noble, Waterstones and other bookstores;

– Join us on Facebook and Twitter for updates on our publications and news about our authors;

– Visit our site www.glagoslav.com to check out our Catalogue and subscribe to our Newsletter.

Glagoslav Publications is getting ready to release a new collection and planning some interesting surprises — stay with us to find out!

Glagoslav Publications
Office 36, 88-90 Hatton Garden
EC1N 8PN London, UK
Tel: + 44 (0) 20 32 86 99 82
Email: contact@glagoslav.com

Glagoslav Publications Catalogue

- The Time of Women by Elena Chizhova
- Sin by Zakhar Prilepin
- Hardly Ever Otherwise by Maria Matios
- Khatyn by Ales Adamovich
- Christened with Crosses by Eduard Kochergin
- The Vital Needs of the Dead by Igor Sakhnovsky
- A Poet and Bin Laden by Hamid Ismailov
- Kobzar by Taras Shevchenko
- White Shanghai by Elvira Baryakina
- The Stone Bridge by Alexander Terekhov
- King Stakh's Wild Hunt by Uladzimir Karatkevich
- Depeche Mode by Serhii Zhadan
- Herstories, An Anthology of New Ukrainian Women Prose Writers
- The Battle of the Sexes Russian Style by Nadezhda Ptushkina
- A Book Without Photographs by Sergey Shargunov
- Sankya by Zakhar Prilepin
- Wolf Messing by Tatiana Lungin
- Good Stalin by Victor Erofeyev
- Solar Plexus by Rustam Ibragimbekov
- Don't Call me a Victim! by Dina Yafasova
- A History of Belarus by Lubov Bazan
- Children's Fashion of the Russian Empire by Alexander Vasiliev
- Boris Yeltsin - The Decade that Shook the World by Boris Minaev
- A Man Of Change - A study of the political life of Boris Yeltsin
- Gnedich by Maria Rybakova
- Marina Tsvetaeva - The Essential Poetry
- Multiple Personalities by Tatyana Shcherbina
- The Investigator by Margarita Khemlin
- Leo Tolstoy – Flight from paradise by Pavel Basinsky
- Moscow in the 1930 by Natalia Gromova
- Prisoner by Anna Nemzer
- Alpine Ballad by Vasil Bykau
- The Complete Correspondence of Hryhory
- The Tale of Aypi by Ak Welsapar
- Selected Poems by Lydia Grigorieva
- The Fantastic Worlds of Yuri Vynnychuk

More coming soon…

www.ingramcontent.com/pod-product-compliance
Lightning Source LLC
Chambersburg PA
CBHW031120080526
44587CB00011B/1050